WELFARE IN THE KANTIAN STATE

Welfare in
the Kantian State

ALEXANDER KAUFMAN

OXFORD
UNIVERSITY PRESS

Oxford University Press, Great Clarendon Street, Oxford OX2 6DP

Oxford New York
Athens Auckland Bangkok Bogotá Buenos Aires Calcutta
Cape Town Chennai Dar es Salaam Delhi Florence Hong Kong Istanbul
Karachi Kuala Lumpur Madrid Melbourne Mexico City Mumbai
Nairobi Paris São Paulo Singapore Taipei Tokyo Toronto Warsaw
and associated companies in Berlin Ibadan

Oxford is a registered trade mark of Oxford University Press

Published in the United States
by Oxford University Press Inc., New York

British Library Cataloguing in Publication Data
Data available

Library of Congress Cataloging in Publication Data

Kaufman, Alexander.
Welfare in the Kantian State / Alexander Kaufman.
Includes bibliographical references and index.
1. Kant, Immanuel, 1724–1804—Contributions in political science.
2. Kant, Immanuel, 1724–1804—Contributions in the concept of justice.
3. Welfare state. I. Title.
JC181.K4K38 1999 320'.01'1—dc21 98-43149
ISBN 0-19-829467-0

1 3 5 7 9 10 8 6 4 2

Typeset in 10 on 12pt Times
by Best-set Typesetter Ltd., Hong Kong
Printed in Great Britain
on acid-free paper by
Bookcraft (Bath) Ltd
Midsomer Norton, Someset

To my family, especially Nomi

ACKNOWLEDGEMENTS

While writing this book, I have received invaluable advice and support from many people. I would particularly like to thank Bernard Manin, who has read and commented on the book through several drafts. Bernard advised me throughout my graduate education at the University of Chicago, and taught me much of what I know about political philosophy. I owe a special debt of gratitude to Patrick Riley, who introduced me not only to the study of Kant's political philosophy, but, in addition, to his own important and influential account of Kantian politics. My work with Riley at Harvard, in the late 1980s, provided the initial impetus for this project. I would also like to acknowledge my debt to Christine Korsgaard, whose illuminating seminars on the *Groundwork*, the *Second Critique*, and the *Metaphysics of Morals* profoundly influenced my understanding of these works. I owe a tremendous intellectual debt to John Rawls, whose work has changed the nature of Kantian scholarship in the last quarter of the twentieth century. Special thanks are also due to Henry Allison, Daniel Brudney, Ted Cohen, Jon Elster, Russell Hardin, Stephen Holmes, Martha Nussbaum, Robert Pippin, and Susan Shell, all of whom have been generous in their comments and criticisms.

Finally, I would like to thank my family, without whose patience and support, my research could not have been completed. In particular my wife, Nomi, has altruistically supported my seemingly endless research enterprise. My children, Jonah and Dafna, have encouraged me through their interest in 'my book'. Finally, I would like to thank my parents for their unflagging and invaluable moral support.

A.K.

CONTENTS

CONTENTS

ABBREVIATIONS AND NOTE ON TRANSLATIONS

References to and citations of Kant's works are given parenthetically in the text using the following abbreviations, and for most works citing the page numbers of the relevant volume of *Kants gesammelte Schriften* (published by the *Preussische Akademie der Wissenschaften*, Berlin). The volume numbers are listed at the end of the entries below. The *Critique of Pure Reason* is cited by the page numbers of the A and B editions. Citations from *The Contest of the Faculties*, 'On the Common Saying: "This May be True in Theory, But it does not Apply in Practice"', *Religion within the Limits of Reason Alone*, 'Towards Perpetual Peace', and 'What is Orientation in Thinking' are cited only by the page number of the translation.

CF *The Conflict of the Faculties* (1798), Second Part trans. H.B. Nisbet, in Hans Reiss (ed.) *Kant's Political Writings* (Cambridge: Cambridge University Press, 1970). (vii)

CPR *Critique of Pure Reason* (1st edn. 1781, 2nd edn. 1787), trans. Norman Kemp Smith (New York: St Martin's Press, 1965). (iii, iv)

CPr *Critique of Practical Reason* (1788), trans. Lewis White Beck (New York: Macmillan, The Library of Liberal Arts, 1956). (v)

CJ *Critique of Judgment* (1790), trans. Werner S. Pluhar (Indianapolis: Hackett, 1987). (v)

DV *The Doctrine of Virtue (Tugendlehre)* (1797), trans. Mary Gregor as *Metaphysical First Principles of the Doctrine of Virtue*, in *The Metaphysics of Morals* (Cambridge: Cambridge University Press, 1991). (vi)

FI *First Introduction to the Critique of Judgment*, trans. Werner H. Pluhar, in *Critique of Judgment* (Indianapolis: Hackett, 1987). (xx)

G *Grounding of the Metaphysics of Morals* (1785), trans. James W. Ellington (Indianapolis: Hackett, 1983). (vi)

GTPP   'Uber den Gebrauch Teleologischer Prinzipien in der Philosophie' (1788). (viii)

LE   *Lectures on Ethics* (1762–93). Drawn from the lecture notes of Johann Gottlieb Herder, Georg Ludwig Collins, Chr. Mongrovius, and Johann Friedrich Vigilantius by Peter Heath and J. B. Schneewind, trans. Peter Heath (Cambridge: Cambridge University Press, 1997). (xxvii, xxix)

MJ   *The Metaphysical Principles of Justice (Rechtslehre)* (1797), trans. Mary Gregor as *Metaphysical First Principles of the Doctrine of Right*, in *The Metaphysics of Morals* (Cambridge: Cambridge University Press, 1991). (vi)

R   *Religion within the Limits of Reason Alone* (1793), trans. Theodore M. Greene and Hoyt H. Hudson (La Salle, Ill.: Open Court, 1934; repr. New York: Harper Torchbooks, 1960). (vi)

TP   'On the Common Saying: "This May Be True in Theory, but it does not Apply in Practice"' (1793), trans. H. B. Nisbet, in Hans Reiss (ed.), *Kant's Political Writings* (Cambridge: Cambridge University Press, 1970). (viii)

TPP   'Towards Perpetual Peace' (1795), trans. H. B. Nisbet, in Hans Reiss (ed.), *Kant's Political Writings* (Cambridge: Cambridge University Press, 1970). (viii)

WE   'What is Enlightenment?' (1784), trans. H. B. Nisbet, in Hans Reiss (ed.), *Kant's Political Writings* (Cambridge: Cambridge University Press, 1970). (viii)

WOT   'What is Orientation in Thinking?' (1786), trans. H. B. Nisbet, in Hans Reiss (ed.), *Kant's Political Writings*, 2nd edn. (Cambridge: Cambridge University Press, 1970, 1991). (viii)

Note: The use of the masculine for non-gender-specific pronouns reflects house style and not the ideology of the author.

INTRODUCTION

This study explores two themes, *Kant* and *social welfare*, with a particular emphasis on issues relating to poverty and inequality. In exploring these two themes, I attempt to specify the implications of Kantian theory for the state's responsibility to assist the least advantaged.

I have focused specifically on *Kantian* normative theory for four reasons. First, I believe Kantian politics offers a promising basis for a theory of social welfare. Justice, for Kant, is a state of affairs which makes possible the realization of the right to freedom 'belonging to every man by virtue of his humanity'. Kant defines freedom as 'independence from being constrained by another's choice' (MJ 237). Thus, Kant's account of justice might be expected to ground an indictment of forms of civil condition which fail to protect individuals from exploitation and coercion.

Second, Kant's political writings address what I believe to be the fundamental question in applied political theory: how should the formal requirements of justice be realized in positive law and public policy? Kant's response to this question is, admittedly, complex and problematic. Nevertheless, Kant offers a most determined and original effort to address this problem.

Third, Kant's political thought has been misappropriated by libertarian thinkers, such as Wilhelm von Humboldt and Friedrich Hayek, who claim that Kantian theory limits the legitimate role of the state to classic liberalism's night watchman. Proponents of this libertarian interpretation ground their claims in: (i) the assertion that, for Kant, 'juridical laws . . . are essentially negative and limiting principles which merely restrict our exercise of freedom' (Hayek 1976: 43); and (ii) Kant's explicit rejection of happiness as an appropriate ground for legislation. The libertarian interpretation, which has influenced the thought of such disparate philosophers as Michael Oakeshott and Robert Nozick, remains the dominant account of Kantian politics among continental scholars. The profound political influence of this libertarian interpretation of Kant, may, to a significant degree, explain the regressive light in which many continental thinkers have viewed liberalism. I argue that such libertarian interpretations inflate Kant's concerns with contingency and paternalism, and exaggerate the degree to which Kant insists upon the negative character of juridical law, thus distorting and misrepresenting Kant's arguments.

It is important to note that the dominance of the libertarian interpretation is a recent phenomenon. In the late nineteenth and early twentieth centuries, the 'left' Kantianism of the Marburg school, particularly as embodied in the work of Hermann Cohen and his student Karl Vorlander, was extremely influential.[1] Cohen (1910) asserts that Kant's argument for a duty to respect humanity as an end, and not merely a means, grounds a direct indictment of capitalist economic relations.[2] Vorlander extends Cohen's analysis, arguing that insights derivable from Kant's ethical theory could ground 'a Kantian socialist ethics' (Van Der Linden 1988: 296). The Marburg school's interpretation of Kant has continued to influence political theorists of the left, notably Eduard Bernstein (1961) and Lucien Goldman (1971), both of whom argue directly from the duty to respect humanity as an end to indictments of capitalist economic and social relations.

While right-Kantians exaggerate the degree to which Kant's categorical distinction between ethical and political legislation constrains the appropriate content of public right, left-Kantians, symmetrically, virtually ignore Kant's distinction between ethical and political duty, arguing directly from ethical principles to political conclusions. Thus, right-Kantians are more faithful than left-Kantians to the *form* of Kant's argument; right-Kantians' insistence on an extreme reading of Kant's account of juridical law, however,

---

[1] The editors of *Kant-Studien* introduced Vorlander (1902) with a note stating that '[t]he neo-Kantian movement in socialism has gained in the past few years such a significance that the editors of *Kant-Studien* feel obliged to keep their readers informed about this movement' (Vorlander 1902: 23 n.; cited in Van Der Linden 1988: 291). Other influential members of the Marburg school included Max Adler, Kurt Eisner, Albert Gorland, Paul Natorp, Alfredo Poggi, and Franz Staudinger. See Van Der Linden's (1988) helpful discussion of the Marburg school and its influence (291–307).

[2] See Van Der Linden's (1988) helpful discussion of Cohen's argument (205–39).

obscures substantive implications of Kant's political thought that left-Kantians more plausibly develop.

A satisfactory Kantian theory of social welfare must develop these substantive implications while respecting the Recht/Tugend distinction that grounds Kant's division of his *Metaphysics of Morals*. My analysis presupposes Kant's argument for this division and argues that Kant's account of public right, as narrowly circumscribed in the *Rechtslehre*, nevertheless indicates that the realization of a rightful civil condition requires the adoption of certain kinds of social welfare legislation.

Finally, contemporary communitarians argue that Kantian theories of justice are necessarily grounded in a conception of 'an antecedently individuated subject, standing always at a certain distance from the interests it has'. Such a conception of the self, it is argued, 'put[s] the self beyond the reach of experience,' and therefore 'rules out the possibility that common purposes and ends could . . . define a community in the constitutive sense' (Sandel 1982: 62). In response to this criticism, I will attempt to demonstrate that a developed account of Kantian political justice is necessarily articulated through a direct engagement with relations in experience. Kantian political judgment takes relations in experience as unfiltered inputs and generates an account of social goals grounded in the intersubjective judgments of members of the community (the *sensus communis*). Thus, Kantian political judgment is not grounded in deliberations 'beyond the reach of experience', and, in fact, generates an account of 'common purposes and ends' which are constituted by the collective judgments of members of the community as a whole. Since these purposes and ends derive from the collective intersubjective judgments of members of the community, they are well suited to 'define a community in the constitutive sense'.

Thus, my research is not limited to exegesis. Rather, I intend my work to be both corrective and exploratory. I argue against the libertarian interpretation of Kant in order to correct the impression that Kantian political theory, perhaps the central theory of rights in the liberal tradition, severely limits state authority to aid the disadvantaged. I argue for a closer investigation of Kantian political theory because I believe that Kant's thought offers an important and fruitful framework for justifying state intervention and refining our understanding of the goals of social welfare policy.

1

Kant and Welfare

KANT defines 'justice' or 'right' as the set of conditions under which individuals can coexist freely (MJ 230). Such free coexistence can only be sustained, Kant argues, in civil society under public law reflecting the united will of the people. Since Kant defines freedom as 'independence from being constrained by another's choice' (MJ 237), his account of right might appear to ground an indictment of forms of civil condition which fail to guarantee freedom from inherently coercive or exploitative economic conditions. If institutional features of civil society constitute severe obstacles to the exercise of man's innate right to freedom, then collective action to mitigate such obstacles would seem not merely permissible, but required.

A traditional interpretation, however, holds that Kant's political philosophy is limited to the investigation of 'the formal compatibility of the external freedom of one person with that of others' (Kersting 1992*b*: 345).[1] This focus on formal compatibility limits Kant's account of justice to an account of the constraints which reason places on the state's authority to regulate external action.

If individuals are to coexist freely, the traditional interpretation follows Kant in arguing, the exercise of freedom must be regulated by coercive laws. Otherwise, the free acts of one individual could always operate to constrain the freedom of another individual (MJ 231, 232, 307, 312). The doctrine of right is thus 'the sum of those laws for which an external lawgiving is possible' (MJ 229).

If right is to secure conditions ensuring external liberty, however, all members of civil society must acknowledge the binding nature of principles of right. Any claim of a right to possess and use property, for example, implicitly asserts that all others are obligated to restrict their external actions to conform to the

---

[1] See also Kersting (1992*a*); Mulholland (1990); Pogge (1988); Weinrib (1987); Williams (1983).

claimed right. This claim, however, involves 'acknowledging that I am in turn under obligation to every other to refrain from using what is externally his' (MJ 255). The obligation to respect rights arises from a universal rule governing external relations; therefore, no obligation to respect rights can exist unless each member of civil society is assured that all other members acknowledge and respect such rights (MJ 256).

Thus, the Kantian argument continues, external right can only obligate all members of civil society if it derives from a general, rather than merely unilateral, will. Since: (i) mutual freedom requires enforceable obligations of external right; and (ii) enforceable obligations of external right can only exist within a civil society governed by a general will; therefore (iii) mutual freedom can only exist within a civil society governed by a general will.

Since individuals can only achieve freedom in a civil society governed by a general will, the state can be understood as the product of a hypothetical social contract under which individuals unite into a general will and surrender their natural freedom in order to obtain the more complete freedom of a member of a civil society (MJ 315; TP 73).

The state's legitimacy derives from the need to guarantee mutual external freedom (MJ 315–16); therefore, the state exercises its power legitimately only to the extent that its use of coercive force is necessary to secure external freedom through the enforcement of law (TP 73).[2]

The traditional interpretation takes this argument to establish that Kant's account of right merely defines and limits the kinds of constraints the state may impose in regulating external action. Interpreted in this way, his theory is restricted to an account of the limitations that practical reason imposes on the state's coercive power. Thus, Kant's theory of the state takes on a negative character, describing the limits on state action, and not elaborating the nature of the state's authority to govern. The state's primary responsibility is to secure the negative liberty of its subjects, rather than to achieve improvements in social welfare or happiness.

In addition, Kant's vehement rejection of welfare or happiness as

---

[2] Kant advances two additional criteria for the legitimacy of legislation: (i) compatibility with being made public (TPP 125–6); and (ii) compatibility with what a people may enact for itself as law (TP 85). These criteria constrain the content of legitimate legislation, but do not define the nature of the state's legislative authority.

a ground for legislation (TP 80, 82–3, CF 183 n., MJ 318) appears to
require a libertarian conception of the state. In arguing that juridical legislation must not be grounded in a principle of realizing
happiness or well-being (TP 80, CF 183 n.[3]), libertarian theorists
assert, Kant intends to criticize legislation designed to realize
material goals, such as improvements in public welfare. Libertarian
interpretations of Kantian political theory have, in fact, influenced
the history of political thought by helping to redefine the classic
liberal notion of the state. Humboldt (1969/1852), citing Kant,
argued that the night watchman state was a necessary condition for
the cultivation of autonomy and individuality.[4] In Humboldt's new
classical synthesis, the grounding of the classic liberal conception
of the state shifts from self-preservation to autonomy.[5] Hayek's
(1976) influential indictment of the interventionist welfare state
explicitly acknowledges its debt to the traditional interpretation:
'[Kant] saw more clearly than most later philosophers of law
that . . . "juridical laws [must] abstract altogether from our ends,
they are essentially negative and limiting principles which merely
restrict our exercise of freedom" ' (Hayek 1976: 43).

Thus, the traditional interpretation of Kant's thought has remained influential, and grounded a reinterpretation of the classic
liberal state by theorists such as Humboldt and Hayek. Yet much
in Kant's political and moral philosophy is inconsistent with this
reading.

In particular, a salient strand of Kant's political thought develops a richer and more positive account of right. Politics, in this
account, must be guided by morality: '[a] true system of politics

---

[3] 'No generally valid principle of legislation can be based on happiness' (TP 80).
Legislation grounded in a principle of improving the material well-being of the
subjects 'depends . . . upon the will's *material* aspect, which is empirical and thus
incapable of becoming a universal rule' (CF 183 n.).

[4] 'The cultivation of the understanding . . . is generally achieved by [man's] own
activity, his own ingenuity, or his own methods of using the discoveries of others.
Now, State measures always imply more or less compulsion; and even when this
is not the case, they accustom men to look for instruction, guidance, and assistance
from without . . . whether it coerces the citizen by some compulsory arrangement . . . or by . . . rewards, and other encouragements attractive to him . . . [the
state] will always deviate very far from the best system of instruction. For this
unquestionably consists in proposing, as it were, all possible solutions of the problem in question, so that the citizen may select, according to his own judgment, the
course which seems to him the most appropriate' (Humboldt 1969/1852: 19).

[5] 'Humboldt gives traditional liberal theory nothing less than a fresh rationale'
(Rosenblum 1987: 17).

cannot . . . take a single step without first paying tribute to moral-ity' (TPP 125). This 'tribute to morality' requires the realization of a concrete political end, the 'highest political good'. The realization of this end is the 'entire final end of the doctrine of Right' (MJ 355). Moreover, the realization of this political purpose is 'a *moral task* . . . a state of affairs which must arise out of recognising one's duty' (TPP 122). Such an account of a politics grounded in the moral duty to realize a positive end (the highest political good) appears inconsistent with the libertarian assertion that Kantian right must consist of merely negative and limiting principles that abstract altogether from ends.

While offering a promising basis for a positive account of justice, Kant's political teleology also suggests an apparent inconsistency within Kant's political theory: Kant argues that self-legislation must be grounded in a formal principle (CPr 30–1, CF 184), but Kant's political teleology appears to require that the individual should ground his choices in a material principle (the desire to realize the highest political good). Thus, Kant's account of political teleology appears to be in tension with his account of moral legislation. This apparent tension dissipates upon more care-ful investigation, however, since Kant does not argue that individ-uals should ground their choices in the *desire* to realize the highest political good. Rather, the highest political good is a system of objective ends each of which the agent has a *duty* to realize. The systematic organization of these ends operates as a heuristic, revealing practical implications which are less salient when ends associated with obligatory maxims are viewed separately. It is in this sense that Kant's description of moral philosophy[6] as 'a pure practical teleology'[7] (GTPP 182–3) seems most plausible.

Kant's political teleology is therefore plausibly seen as consistent with his account of moral legislation. While involving a set of complex and potentially problematic claims that must be inter-preted with great care, political teleology nevertheless constitutes a potentially valuable resource in developing the positive dimensions of Kant's political thought. In particular, an examination of Kantian political teleology may yield insights regarding the relation

---

[6] Moral philosophy includes both right (*Recht*) and virtue (*Tugend*). Kant's claim (that moral philosophy is a practical teleology) thus includes the claim that right, or political philosophy, is a practical teleology.

[7] '[E]ine reine praktische Teleologie' (GTPP 182–3).

between Kant's rejection of consequentialism in the *Rechtslehre* and his simultaneous arguments in favour of positive state interventions designed to improve social welfare, such as income support for the poor (MJ 326), a system of state-funded health care (MJ 367), and a universal, state-funded, system of public education (CF 188–9). In this study, I will evaluate the status of this teleological strand of Kant's political thought, and assess the resources it supplies for a Kantian theory of social welfare.

I will argue that the traditional interpretation succeeds neither as a faithful reading of Kant's texts nor as a critical reconstruction of Kantian political theory. Rather, I will argue that Kant's political theory articulates a conception of the state's role that is fully consistent with, and in fact requires, a well-developed theory of social welfare.

Four objections to a Kantian theory of social welfare are central in the traditional interpretation of Kant's theory of right. First, Kant's analysis of the metaphysical ground of natural law appears to impose severe constraints on the legitimate activities of the state. Second, even if these constraints do not bar state welfare interventions, Kantian politics seems to offer no basis for determining the substance of such a policy, since positive law is necessarily contingent (MJ 227). Third, several salient passages in Kant's political writings appear to suggest that political progress is to be realized through the 'mechanism of nature', and not through a positive legislative agenda.

Finally, Kant explicitly and repeatedly rejects 'welfare' as a principle of legislation. Since this fourth objection has been widely influential, and has inspired a large body of literature, I will defer discussion of the issue to Chapter 2, which will focus entirely on Kant's rejection of the 'welfare' principle.

The first three objections appear plausible because Kant's major statement of his political theory develops only the metaphysical principles of right. The constraint which these principles exercise over the content of positive law is not well specified.

In section 1, I will examine these three objections, which have traditionally been understood to bar a substantial Kantian theory of social welfare. In section 2, I will examine Kant's explicit treatment of welfare in his political works, and argue that this treatment suggests a plausible basis for a theory of social welfare.

1. METAPHYSICAL ANALYSIS, INDETERMINACY, AND THE CUNNING OF NATURE

In this section, I will argue that: (i) Kant's metaphysical account of natural law does not necessarily ground a unique set of constraints on relations in experience; that nevertheless, (ii) Kant argues for a political theory which is sufficiently well specified to ground policy determinations; and that (iii) the realization of moral ends in Kantian politics requires morally motivated activity.

A. *The Metaphysical Analysis: Justice as the Restriction of Legitimate Forms of Coercion*

Analysis conducted at the level of metaphysical principles examines the relations of general concepts, independent of the consideration of contingent objects and relations in experience (see CJ 181). Presenting his analysis at this level of abstraction allows Kant to develop his political theory as an extension and elaboration of his ethical theory, which is a theory of pure principles, and to argue for principles which apply necessarily and universally.

In the *Metaphysics of Morals*, Kant attempts to derive from the supreme moral principle of the *Groundwork* an account of the metaphysical principles which ground the normativity of internal and external legislation. In the *Rechtslehre*, Kant's specific goal is to ground the obligation to obey laws which govern external acts. Since external laws are the subject of positive legislation, Kant must provide an account of the normativity of natural law which grounds the obligation to obey positive law.

In order to demonstrate that a metaphysical analysis can ground principles governing relations in experience, however, Kant requires an argument establishing that rational principles have normative implications for relations in experience. Kant addresses this problem by 'considering objects of choice and determining, to the extent possible in "metaphysical first principles", what rights human beings have or can acquire' (Gregor 1991: 23).

Kant's argument develops insights derived from his consideration of the relation of two general concepts: the notion of possession of an external object; and the idea of freedom. First, Kant defines right as 'the sum of the conditions under which the choice of one can be united with the choice of another in accordance with a

universal law of freedom' (MJ 230). Since the doctrine of right is
to derive principles from the categorical imperative, Kant justifies
the centrality of freedom in his account of right simply by noting
that '*[f]reedom* (independence of being constrained by another's
choice) . . . is the only original right belonging to every man by
virtue of his *humanity*' (MJ 237, second emphasis mine). This original right is thus grounded directly in the categorical imperative's
requirement to 'treat humanity . . . always at the same time as an
end, and never simply as a means' (G 429).

Since all humans possess the right to external freedom, the fundamental principle of right is therefore the principle that '[a]ny
action is right if by it or its maxim the freedom of choice of each can
coexist with everyone's freedom in accordance with universal law'
(MJ 230). This principle implicitly authorizes exercises of state
coercive power which are necessary 'as hindering a hindrance to
freedom' (MJ 231).

Second, Kant argues that the will can make no law forbidding the
use of what is usable. Any other conclusion would lead to a contradiction. The use of any object, consistent with the free use of
objects by others, is consistent with the fundamental principle of
right. If a positive law proscribes the use of such an object, such
a use is both right (in accordance with the universal principle of
right) and not right (contrary to positive law) simultaneously (see
Gregor 1988: 774 ff.).

Finally, Kant argues, if the possibility of rightful possession is a
necessary correlate of the first principle of right, then right authorizes the use of coercion to protect such rightful possession. Thus, 'a
further condition is necessary to insure that one's choice will be
compatible with the outer freedom of every other' (Gregor 1988:
776). This condition is not satisfied simply through the existence of
an outer coercive authority to protect rights. Rather, rightful possession can only exist in a condition in which all are assured that
their rightful possession will be protected. Thus, rightful possession
can only exist when the will of all is constituted into a general will
within a civil society. Under the reciprocal system of obligations
which define civil society, 'anyone who asserts a right to an object
acknowledges that he is in turn bound' to respect rightful possession by others (Gregor 1988: 779). One gives this assurance only by
consenting to submit to an external coercive authority.

Thus, by analysing the relation of the categorical imperative to the general concept of possession of an object, Kant grounds the coercive authority of the state. Kant's analysis grounds this coercive authority in the necessity of protecting property rights.

This argument appears to establish that the formal principle of right does in fact necessarily constrain relations in experience. The argument has been taken to impose very strict constraints on the role of the state in Kantian political theory. Thus, for example Murphy (1970) argues that a principled Kantian position should require 'that it is unjust to tax Jones in order to be benevolent to Smith' (144). Such a serious invasion of individual property rights should be justified only in order to '[hinder] a hindrance to freedom', the sole legitimate justification for exercises of coercive force by the state.

In fact, while a narrow interpretation of this argument restricts state functions to securing the conditions necessary to ensure the possibility of rightful possession, such an interpretation is not dictated by Kant's argument. Kant merely argues that rightful possession must be possible and that the state must guarantee this possibility. Kant presents a wide range of state powers as consistent with this property argument. For example, Kant argues that the sovereign has the authority to administer the economy (MJ 325); to provide income support to the poor (MJ 326); and to provide a system of public education (CF 188–9).

Kant's argument that rightful possession of property must be possible does not, in fact, appear to require that the state protect any particular allocation of property. Rather, rights are 'apportioned' (*erteilend*) to members of civil society by the sovereign (MJ 316): under principles of right, 'determination of the particular property of each is in accordance with the necessary formal principle of *division (Einteilung)* . . . instead of with principles of *aggregation (Aggregation)* (which proceeds empirically from the parts to the whole)' (MJ 323–4).

While Kant discusses the idea of original acquisition as a hypothetical basis for claims to possession in the state of nature, he states clearly that *all* claims to property originating in the state of nature are merely 'provisional' (MJ 256–7, 263–4). It is central to his argument that civil society must exist *before* conclusive right-claims can be established.

Each individual in civil society has 'relinquished entirely' his presocial freedom, and therefore his provisional rights,[8] in order to take up the rights apportioned to him within civil society (MJ 316): 'all [conclusive] rights [to private property] must be derived from the sovereign as . . . the supreme proprietor' (MJ 323). In order to maintain the security and rightful condition of civil society, the sovereign must retain the authority to employ property to address the needs of civil society and its members (MJ 311, 324–7).

Thus, the state does not merely endorse provisional property holdings deriving from original acquisition in the state of nature. Rather, the state must allocate property in such a way that a rightful condition of civil society is achieved and maintained (MJ 311, 315–16, 323–4). The sovereign must, therefore, allocate property according to a just distributive principle. Specification of the nature and content of this principle must constitute the core of Kant's discussion of public right. While Kant does not define such a principle explicitly, I will argue, in section 2, that his concern to define such a principle is reflected throughout 'Public Right'.

B. *Indeterminacy of Positive Law*

The argument for the normativity of natural law requires the protection of property in general, but provides no articulated basis for specifying the form of property holdings which the state must protect. Thus, Kant might appear to have simply derived a new general principle which cannot be constitutive for experience.

Such potential indeterminacy has grounded concerns regarding the 'content problem' in Kantian ethics and politics (see Williams 1985: 68–9; Sandel 1982: 172–3). An effective response to this criticism must demonstrate that a more specific interpretation of the property argument, with substantive implications, is possible within the terms of Kant's analysis. In Chapters 4 and 5, I will argue for an account of political judgment addressing the content problem.

While this Hegelian criticism is intended to demonstrate a general failing of Kant's moral and political philosophy, some Kantians have embraced the indeterminacy of positive law as an inevitable and acceptable feature of Kantian politics. For example, Gregor

[8] Since all provisional rights are grounded in the innate right to freedom. '[T]he concept of rightful possession is a concept of freedom . . . To say that I am in rightful possession of an external object is to assert that anyone who uses it without my consent infringes on my freedom' (Gregor 1988: 774).

(1991), expressing a view common in the literature (see Pogge 1988: 417; Sullivan 1989: 249; Kersting 1992*a*: 151; Byrd 1993: 46), argues that 'public laws are positive laws, the content of which is contingent and chosen by a legislator who is the author of the law' (13).

If the content of positive legislation, in general, is merely contingent, then it will not be possible to argue that certain categories of legislation are rationally necessary; the power to determine the legislative agenda is thus defined as the prerogative of the legislator. Moreover, members of civil society lack a standpoint from which to criticize the content of legislation, as long as it is consistent with the most basic requirements of the metaphysical principles of right.

Gregor does not, however, argue that positive law is entirely contingent in its content: 'What laws the legislator enacts will depend on contingent circumstances and cannot be specified a priori, *but* they will embody the principles established in "Private Right" ' (16, emphasis mine). Gregor follows Kant explicitly in requiring that positive legislation must 'embody' the principles of right.[9] Yet the relation between natural and positive law is ambiguous and underspecified.

Kant argues that: (i) institutions consistent with the metaphysical principles of right are essential preconditions for the realization of freedom; and (ii) 'it is only in conformity with the conditions of freedom and equality that [a] people can become a state and enter into a civil constitution' (MJ 315). But what if the sovereign fails to act to realize any of the conditions necessary to ensure freedom and equality? According to Gregor's indeterminacy argument, the sovereign possesses almost complete power to determine the legislative agenda. Moreover, the legislator possesses an empirical, not a purely rational will: we cannot assume that the legislator will act from rational principles. If: (i) right requires a civil condition in which 'the conditions of freedom and equality' are embodied; and (ii) certain legislation and institutional arrangements are necessary conditions of the realization of such conditions; then (iii) right requires the satisfaction of such necessary conditions. Unless natural law constrains the legislative agenda, however, Kant provides

---

[9] 'It is the form of a state as such, that is, *of the state as Idea* ... [that] serves as a norm for every actual union into a commonwealth (hence serves as a norm for its internal constitution)' (MJ 313).

no account of the satisfaction of such necessary conditions. Thus, the indeterminacy argument creates a serious discontinuity in Kantian right.

Moreover, as Gregor acknowledges, this notion of almost complete contingency of positive law is inconsistent with Kant's arguments in the *Rechtslehre* that the sovereign must 'give its laws in accordance with principles of Private Right and . . . bring the form of the state into accord with the Idea of the original contract' (Gregor 1991: 16).

In fact, the indeterminacy argument may confuse contingency of form with contingency of content. Kant does state that positive law is 'contingent' (MJ 227). But this point appears to be descriptive, rather than normative. Positive law derives from the contingent will of the legislator, and is thus formally contingent: it is not established by some purely rational process. Thus, Kant contrasts 'contingent and chosen' legislation with legislation 'that binds us a priori and unconditionally by our own reason' (MJ 227).

Yet the fact that legislation is chosen by an empirical will does not mean that the legislation is not subject to substantive requirements deriving from pure reason. Unless empirical wills are subject to requirements derived from pure reason, Kantian morality can exercise no constraint over the merely empirical wills of human beings. Thus, if we accept the claim that positive law is *necessarily* contingent merely because it derives from the empirical will of a legislator, then we must abandon the hope that the pure principles of morality can constrain a merely mortal will.

Weinrib (1987, 1992) presents a more general argument for the claim that Kantian right is essentially indeterminate. Rather than grounding his claims in a construal of Kant's explicit arguments, Weinrib argues that indeterminacy is an intrinsic feature of a conceptual account of right, such as Kant's.

Weinrib argues that legality, in Kant, has the status of an *idea*. Ideas unify the understanding's concepts of objects by exhibiting the connection of these concepts under a single principle which expresses their systematic relation.[10] Thus, for example, reason

---

[10] Ideas 'unif[y] the manifold of concepts . . . [by] positing a certain collective unity as the goal of the activities of the understanding' (A644/B672). Reason seeks 'to exhibit the connection of its parts in conformity with a single principle. This unity of reason always presupposes an idea, namely the form of a whole of knowledge' (A645/B673).

requires an idea of the 'fundamental power' underlying the various faculties of the human mind (sensation, consciousness, imagination, etc.) in order to arrive at a systematic representation of human mental powers (A649/B677).

Kant does not explicitly characterize legality as an idea. Weinrib notes, however, that several central notions in Kant's legal philosophy are characterized as ideas (the state, the original contract, the sovereign as supreme proprietor, the general will, the civil constitution; see MJ 313–14, 315, 323, 326, 372). Weinrib suggests that these concepts are collectively unified under a fundamental idea of right, or legality.

Weinrib's claim is, in fact, persuasive, since: (i) Kant characterizes each of these subsidiary elements as necessary for the realization of mutual external freedom under universal law; and (ii) Kant characterizes legality as articulating the totality of conditions under which mutual external freedom under universal law can be realized (MJ 230). Reason requires that we seek to unify related principles under a fundamental idea (see A322–3/B378–9, A644/B672). Since the idea of legality exhibits the connection of all concepts subsumable under the concept of right, Weinrib argues, the full realization of the actuality of mutual external freedom must be identical with the full actualization of the idea of legality.

Since legality is a universal concept, it does not ground unique determinations regarding contingent particulars. Thus, no determinate account of the concept of legality can be given a priori, and 'indeterminacy is a necessary aspect of Kant's legal conceptualism' (Weinrib 1987: 505). Thus, Kant's conception of legality cannot specify 'in advance the solution to every controversy' (506).

Yet it is not clear what form of indeterminacy Weinrib's argument identifies. Weinrib is certainly correct in arguing that, for Kant, a pure concept or idea cannot instantiate itself independent of sensible impressions. Thus, the idea of legality will not ground a determination of the specific content of positive law in the absence of intuitions of the empirical circumstances in which the law is to apply (including cultural tradition; resource and technology constraints; existing distribution of wealth; etc.).

Weinrib, however, appears to argue for a stronger form of indeterminacy: the content of the idea of legality is, in many or most cases, *only* rendered determinate when existing legal institutions resolve particular controversies by issuing new (and contingent) determinations of law.[11] In this sense, the content of the idea of legality for a particular society would be radically historically contingent.

In arguing that ideas generally do not have a necessary application to contingent particulars, however, Weinrib appears to go beyond a defensible Kantian claim. Weinrib's argument initially appears to be contradicted by explicit Kantian text, since Kant argues that, for a pure concept which is unproblematically given ('certain in itself'), 'only *judgment* is required to execute the process of subsumption, and the particular is thereby determined in a necessary manner' (A646/B674). Thus, once the contingent particular is given, judgment operates on that particular with 'apodeictic' certainty.

Since the concepts of the metaphysical elements of right are not problematic, it might seem that these concepts should ground determinate judgments subsuming any given particulars. The cited passage, however, characterizes theoretical ideas, while the idea of right is practical. Unlike theoretical ideas, which merely realize reason's purpose of 'secur[ing] the unity of the rules of the understanding under principles' (A302/B359), practical ideas have a normative, rather than merely descriptive, bearing on their objects. The normative character of practical judgments affects the nature of the determinations to be made under ideas of practical reason: since practical ideas have a normative bearing on relations in experience, reason requires that we adopt 'the maxim of working incessantly toward' realizing the ends of morally practical reason (MJ 355).

Even if limited to practical ideas, however, the strong form of Weinrib's indeterminacy argument seems problematic. Kant argues that practical ideas and concepts ground *determinate* judgments governing the individual's choice in any contingent set of circumstances. For example, in the *Critique of Practical Reason*, Kant argues that the idea of objects possible through freedom grounds a rational law which is to govern the individual's practical

---

[11] 'The application of legal concepts reveals ... a contingency of particulars. Because the relations governed by the concept of right are external ... their intelligibility can ... depend upon judgments that are socially or historically relative' (506). 'When Kant talks about the general will determining law, he does not mean that practical reason in its external aspect specifies in advance the solution to every controversy, but instead that practical reason ensures that the solution the judge reaches is a juridical one' (Weinrib 1987: 506).

choices (CPr 57 ff.). In the *Rechtslehre,* Kant argues that pure concepts of the metaphysics of morals are connected with 'principles of application' which have precise normative implications regarding the legislation required to regulate external relations in civil society (MJ 217).

These passages do not necessarily require that practical ideas exhaustively predetermine their own instantiation. Pure concepts may not determine exhaustively the application of subordinate concepts to contingent particulars. For example, while the idea of freedom determines the law a moral agent must follow in choosing his maxim of action, several maxims may be permissible under such a law. If several maxims are permissible, the agent's choice of a maxim will be contingently generated by his empirical will. Nevertheless, the practical idea (and the moral law determined in accordance with the idea) *does* significantly narrow the range of permissible choices, and determines what considerations are relevant in justifying a choice under a subordinate principle. Thus, it is not the case that the determination in a contingent set of circumstances is simply indeterminate before the appropriate legal institution reaches a contingent determination. The metaphysical elements of right narrow the legitimate alternatives to a specifiable range.

This relation between higher-order concepts and determinations made under subordinate principles is central to Kant's account of political reasoning. Kant argues for certain metaphysical principles of natural law which must be instantiated in all positive law (legal decisions and legislation). The fundamental question for a Kantian account of politics is the extent to which the principles of natural law constrain or direct determinations under subordinate principles.

Weinrib (1987) asserts that the natural law simply requires that legislation and/or legal decisions have the correct form (that is, 'that the solution that the judge reaches is a juridical one' (506)). The actual content of the legal determination, Weinrib argues, is merely contingent.

In fact, if natural laws are associated with 'principles of application' which govern the application of 'the highest universal principles' to 'objects of experience' (MJ 217), then Kant's arguments seem to require a complex relation between the higher-order principles of right and the lower-order determinations which specify the content of positive law. The basic metaphysical principles of right are universal, but have a determinate bearing on contingently given particulars. Thus, Kant's metaphysics appears to establish a background set of universal principles which exert a normative constraint on legal reasoning.

While these background principles do not necessarily constrain a particular case uniquely, they define the range of determinations consistent with right. It seems, prima facie, that these principles should provide a 'reason to decide in one way or another', to emphasize the parallel to a contemporary strand of legal philosophy.[12] Moreover, if this sketch of the relation between universal principles and particular determinations is correct in broad outline, it seems at least plausible that, for any well-specified set of facts and issues, we should be able to generate an argument specifying a unique determination which correctly balances the relative weight of the relevant principles.

Therefore, not only does the form of Kant's argument not require strong indeterminacy; it seems that the form of Kant's argument could be consistent with a fully determinate specification of legal judgments flowing from universal principles. In order to determine the degree to which (in)determinacy is implicit in Kant's metaphysical account of justice, we require a clear account of the constraint which the metaphysical principles of right exert over the contingent determinations of positive law. How can the substance of this constraint be rendered specific? Is the constraint merely restrictive, or do the metaphysical principles require that positive law have a certain content? The task of a Kantian political theory is to identify and develop the nature of this relation.

Once the principle governing relations between natural and positive law has been specified, this principle may provide the basis for an account of the specific substantive implications of the principles of natural law. In particular, this principle may ground an account of the form of social welfare legislation necessary to realize a rightful social condition. Yet an important strand of Kant's account of right suggests that the set of positive laws embodying the principles of natural law may not include social welfare legislation. While the highest concept in right is 'the act of free choice in

---

[12] See Dworkin's (1977) seminal discussion of the role of principles in legal reasoning.

general' (MJ 218 n.), Kant distinguishes two distinct aspects of the faculty of free choice. *Willkür* constitutes the mere capacity to act according to self-generated rules 'for the sake of some effect foreseen and desired' (Gregor 1991: 5; see MJ 213–14, 226). The freedom to exercise this capacity without external impediment is *external* freedom. *Wille* is the capacity to select principles of action on the basis of their conformity to the moral law (MJ 213–14, 226). *Wille* thus legislates moral maxims, and their associated ends, to *Willkür*. The freedom of *Wille* to determine the ends of the will is *internal* freedom.

Since right regulates external relations to ensure that the free (external) choice of each individual is exercised consistently with the free (external) choice of every other individual, right constitutes the necessary and sufficient condition for the mutually consistent exercise of *external* freedom. *Internal* freedom, however, requires the free and uncoerced internal choice of ends. Right cannot directly promote the realization of internal freedom, since right coercively regulates merely external actions. Kant's division of the *Metaphysics of Morals* reflects this distinction between external and internal freedom. The *Rechtslehre* provides an account of the external legislation necessary to assure mutually compatible external freedom, while the *Tugendlehre* provides an account of the internal legislation necessary to determine the ends of the will in accordance with the requirements of morality.

Since right cannot regulate the internal choice of ends, several commentators have argued that right must merely regulate behaviour without regard to any end except the mere preservation of a civil condition.[13] Social welfare legislation designed to *achieve the end* of improved social welfare, this interpretation asserts, falls within the jurisdiction of right only if, and only to the extent that, the legislation 'contributes to the preservation of a civil society' (Gregor 1995: 31). This constraint would significantly narrow, if not eliminate, the set of legitimate positive laws addressing social welfare needs.

Clearly, Kant *does* require that right regulates merely external acts and not the choice of ends. Yet there is a meaningful distinction between legislation designed to realize ends and legislation

---

[13] Right must be 'indifferent to ends' (Gregor 1991: 39; see Kersting 1992*b*: 345; Williams 1983: 62–3).

requiring the adoption of ends.[14] Legislation designed to realize
particular ends (such as improvements in health care, education, or
standards of living) may, in practical terms, merely regulate external acts. For example, legislation may require employers to pay a
minimum wage or provide health insurance for their employees
without requiring that the employers adopt any particular end.
Thus, Kant argues that the sovereign may, consistently with the
requirements of right, implement policies designed to assure the
availability of: (i) adequate health care (MJ 367); (ii) a system of
public education (CF 188–9); and (iii) minimum income guarantees
for the poor and orphaned (MJ 326). Symmetrically, legislation
designed merely to regulate external acts may nevertheless necessarily serve the realization of particular ends. In particular, Kant
argues that doctrine of right, itself, serves one 'entire final end': the
realization of 'universal and lasting peace' (MJ 355).

If this argument is correct, then positive laws embodying the
principles of natural law can plausibly include some forms of social
welfare legislation. Such legislation may serve the realization of
ends relating to social welfare just in case the legislation does not in
fact coerce individuals to *adopt* any particular ends. The nature of
the social legislation which may be required, however, cannot be
determined until the principle relating natural and positive law has
been identified.

Pogge (1988) argues for an account of Kantian politics which
defines this relation more precisely. Pogge characterizes Kant's
account of justice as a series of constraints on the permissibility of
the forms of legitimate coercive power employable by the state
to ensure the integrity and endurance of a just civil society. Kantian
justice, Pogge argues, is grounded in two formal principles requiring: (i) mutually consistent domains of external freedom; and
(ii) universal rules constraining the freedom of each equally (414).
These two principles, in effect, embody the formal requirements of
natural right. An account of Kantian justice grounded in these two
principles alone would simply restate the account of Kantian right
in Gregor (1988). In addition, however, Pogge argues for a 'material
principle' which further narrows the set of permissible/necessary
elements of positive law: 'the system of constraints ought optimally
to promote the developing and flourishing of reason' (414).

---

[14] While external lawgiving cannot 'bring about someone's setting an end for
himself . . . it may prescribe external actions that lead to an end without the subject
making it his end' (MJ 239).

While, as Pogge concedes, the addition of this third principle still only generates a partial ordering of permissible positive legislation, the principle does begin to suggest the manner in which natural law can constrain positive law. The two formal principles are grounded in the end of securing the necessary conditions of autonomy. The material principle isolates this highest value and suggests positive, rather than merely restrictive, implications for an account of public right. Thus, it is a corollary of the third principle that any system of laws which restricts human freedom 'can be transformed into a less restrictive one' (421).

While Pogge argues for one account of the constraint exerted by natural law on positive law, his argument does not completely resolve the questions arising under the issue of indeterminacy. In particular, no comprehensive methodology is suggested to ground political judgments regarding the relative justice of sets of institutions. At a very fundamental level, the rationality which requires the formation of civil society (to make freedom possible) requires the constitution of certain institutions, legislation, and rights within civil society. Otherwise, civil society may be as unjust as the state of nature. A legitimate state is only possible 'in conformity with the conditions of freedom and equality' (MJ 315). Yet Pogge suggests no approach to defining even the minimum institutional/legislative requirements necessary to ensure just conditions.

In Chapters 4 and 5, I will argue for an account of Kantian political judgment which would define the nature of the relation between the metaphysical principles of right and the contingent determinations of positive law. In this subsection, my aim has been simply to establish that the indeterminacy arguments do not, in themselves, ground any definite and specific conclusions regarding the nature or possibility of a Kantian theory of social welfare.

C. Coordination and the Mechanism of Nature

Even if a proper understanding of the relation between the principles of natural law and positive law allows us to specify the institutional and legislative requirements necessary to ensure a rightful civil condition, Kant seems to present the task of realizing the *positive* ends of the doctrine of right as 'a problem in political technology' (Yovel 1980: 188) to be resolved through a process of 'negative cooperation' (Hoffe 1992: 133) in the pursuit of collective advantage (see TPP 112). Kant, in several salient passages, appears to assert that 'the mechanism of nature' will guarantee the realization of the ends of politics (TPP 108, 113[15]) through a process of mere coordination (TPP 112[16]), and without reliance upon morally motivated legislation or activity (TPP 108, 123[17]). Thus he argues, famously, that even 'a nation of devils' is capable of setting up a state in conformity with the requirements of right (TPP 112). In light of these claims, positive policies designed to achieve material goals, such as improvements in social welfare, might appear to be both unnecessary and inconsistent with the proper realization of a rightful civil condition.

Yet if the ends of right are to be realized through a merely natural mechanism that proceeds without reliance upon morally motivated choice or legislation, how are we to understand Kant's claim that 'it is a *moral task*, totally different from technical problems, to bring about perpetual peace [the highest goal of politics]' (TPP 122)?[18] And in what way can we fulfil 'our duty to work our way towards this goal' (TPP 114)? Moreover, in his account of public right, Kant asserts that the sovereign possesses the authority to implement policies designed to achieve material goals. In particular, the sovereign possesses the authority to administer the economy (MJ 325), to organize a system of public education (CF 188–9), to assure the availability of adequate health care (MJ 367), and to provide income maintenance for the poor (MJ 326).

Is Kant simply inconsistent in his treatment of policies designed to realize material political goals? While Kant's claims regarding coordination and the mechanism of nature might appear inconsist-

[15] 'Perpetual peace is *guaranteed* by no less an authority than the great artist *Nature* herself. The mechanical process of nature visibly exhibits the purposive plan of producing concord among men, even against their will' (TPP 108). '[N]ature guarantees perpetual peace by the actual mechanism of human inclinations' (TPP 114).

[16] '[N]ature comes to the aid of the universal and rational human will, so admirable in itself, but so impotent in practice, and makes use of precisely those self-seeking inclinations in order to do so. It only remains for men to create a good organization for the state ... and to arrange it in such a way that their self-seeking energies are opposed to one another, each thereby neutralising or eliminating the destructive effects of the rest' (TPP 112).

[17] '[M]orality, with regard to its principles of public right ... has the peculiar feature that the less it makes its conduct depend upon the end it envisages ... the more it will in general harmonize with this end' (TPP 123).

[18] In this passage, Kant asserts that the realization of perpetual peace is the moral task of the 'moral politician'. The task is not limited to such politicians, however, since the task is the politician's by virtue of his being a moral person, and not by virtue of his being a politician.

ent with his assertions regarding a moral duty to realize political ends, a careful examination of the 'mechanism of nature', 'coordination', and 'nation of devils' passages suggests that these passages do not require a rejection of morally motivated political activism. In fact, Kant's argument is narrowly focused on a rather different concern: in arguing that the requirements of morally practical reason, in particular the goal of perpetual peace, can be realized in the external world (through mechanism or coordination), Kant is attempting to preserve the moral obligation to realize perpetual peace.

The Mechanism of Nature

While Kant *does* claim that a mechanism of nature guarantees the realization of the highest political good (perpetual peace), the term 'guarantee' is employed in a carefully limited sense. The guarantee that nature provides is 'enough for practical purposes', but is 'not sufficient to enable us to *prophesy* the future theoretically' (TPP 114). Limited in this way, the guarantee clearly performs a specific role in Kant's argument. Since moral aims cannot amount to duties if 'it is . . . demonstrably impossible to fulfill them' (TP 89), there could be no obligation to act to further the goal of perpetual peace if this goal were merely 'an empty chimera' (TPP 114). In grounding the merely practical judgment that actions designed to further perpetual peace are not futile, the guarantee of nature *preserves the obligation* to realize this moral goal. Rather than implying that political ends must be realized merely through the mechanism of nature, the passage is designed to preserve the obligation to act from moral obligation to realize a specific and material political end.[19]

Coordination

Similarly, while Kant argues that a 'good organization for the state' can be secured through the coordination of 'self-seeking inclinations', such coordination merely provides a mechanism in the external world of experience through which the requirements of morally practical reason can be realized. Kant explicitly states that

---

[19] It is a duty for all moral beings 'to promote [perpetual peace] by using the natural mechanism' (TPP 109).

this framework of coordination is to 'be *used by reason* to facilitate the attainment of its own end, the reign of established right' (TPP 113, emphasis mine). Rather than guaranteeing the realization of particular consequences, such coordination merely guarantees 'that right should eventually get the upper hand' (TPP 113). Those who seek to realize a rightful civil condition must, therefore, actively and intentionally utilize this system of coordination in order to 'get the upper hand'. Coordination, thus, constitutes merely the necessary, rather than the sufficient, condition for the realization of the political ends required by morally practical reason.

A Nation of Devils

Finally, Kant's claim that even a nation of devils can solve 'the problem of setting up a state' (TPP 112) also refers to the satisfaction of a necessary, rather than a sufficient, condition for the realization of the political requirements of morally practical reason. Intelligent devils can 'set up' a state in accordance with the formal requirements of right; yet even a lawful constitution, in accordance with the formal requirements of right, will require 'changes for the better ... in order that the constitution may constantly approach the optimum end prescribed by laws of right' (TPP 118). This optimum end is a 'state of affairs which *must arise out of* recognizing one's duty' (TPP 122, emphasis mine). That is, the citizens of such a state must be 'influenced by the mere idea of the law's authority ... so that they will be able to create for themselves a legislation ultimately founded on right' (TPP 118). Since intelligent devils are not influenced by the mere idea of the law's authority, a state of devils could not realize the 'optimum end' prescribed by right. Rather, the realization of this optimum is 'a *moral task*' (TPP 122), and can be achieved only by a nation of moral beings. Thus, a nation of devils can realize the necessary condition of the highest political good (a lawful state), but not the sufficient condition (moral motivation).

The 'mechanism of nature', 'coordination', and 'nation of devils' passages perform a narrowly limited role in Kant's argument. Kant offers these arguments merely to demonstrate the possibility of realizing the requirements of morally practical reason in the sensible world. Thus, for example, Kant's claims regarding the mechanism of nature are merely intended to clarify what 'nature [does] in relation to the end which man's own reason prescribes to him as a duty' (TPP 112).[20] Kant's argument, in these passages, is not that attempts to realize positive political ends are inappropriate, but that, on the contrary, the natural world is receptive to such efforts.

2. SOCIAL WELFARE IN KANT'S POLITICAL THOUGHT

Since the classic objections discussed in section 1 do not appear to require that positive law is indeterminate in a strong sense, or that the contents of positive law are constrained in a manner excluding policies designed to achieve social welfare goals, it seems plausible that Kantian right could encompass a theory of social welfare. I will begin by examining Kant's brief discussion of the sovereign's right to aid the poor in 'Public Right'.

Kant discusses aid to the poor in a controversial passage in the *Rechtslehre*. Many interpreters have understood this passage as merely an elaboration of the requirement to establish and maintain civil society (the 'postulate of public right'): the state must aid the poor to the extent necessary to maintain its own existence (Aune 1979: 157). I will: (i) argue that the passage will not sustain such an interpretation; (ii) examine alternative interpretations in the literature; and (iii) offer a new interpretation of this passage developing the basis, in Kantian right, for a theory of social welfare.

The Rechtslehre Account

Kant argues that the sovereign, as 'supreme commander' of the land, possesses the right to impose taxes to provide a cluster of services, including support for the poor. In this passage, Kant presents several heterogeneous claims. First, he asserts that the sovereign possesses this right 'insofar as he has taken over the duty of the people'. Second, Kant claims that such taxes are necessary 'for [the people's] own preservation'. Third, he states that intervention to aid the poor may be necessary because 'the general will of the people has united itself into a society in order to maintain itself perpetually'. Finally, he states that 'for this end [maintaining itself

---

[20] Similarly, in the *Critique of Judgment*, Kant argues that, while 'man is never more than a link . . . in the chain of natural purposes', nevertheless, nature merely serves to 'prepare man for what he himself can do in order to be a final purpose' (CJ 430–1).

perpetually], it [the general will] has submitted itself to the internal authority of the state *in order to support those members of society who are unable to maintain themselves'* (MJ 326, emphasis mine).

Those who interpret the passage as an elaboration of the first juridical postulate have stressed the second and third claims: the sovereign possesses the right to provide services necessary to 'preserve' and ensure the 'perpetual' existence of civil society. According to this reading, the 'duty of the people' which the sovereign assumes must be the duty to act from the postulate of public right. Kant, it is asserted, argues here from the implicit premiss that one must have a right to do what one has a duty to do. Yet if the sovereign has in fact assumed a *duty* of the people, then it would seem that he should have not merely a right, but an obligation to provide such services.

Moreover, this account does not explain how Kant can claim that the general will has submitted to the authority of the state 'in order to support those . . . unable to maintain themselves'. Murphy (1970) and Williams (1983), who argue that the passage on aid to the poor merely elaborates the postulate of public right, are clearly disturbed by this final claim. Thus, Murphy complains that 'it is very difficult to see what Kant is up to' in advancing this claim (145). Williams asserts that the claim 'reflect[s] a strong paternalist attitude which elsewhere [Kant] strongly rejects' (197).

It is *possible* to read the passage on aid to the poor as consistent with a strongly antisocial welfarist orientation if Kant is understood to argue simply that the provision of these services in general, and aid to the poor in particular, is necessary for the continued existence of civil society. Since the general will *has* united itself in order to ensure the continued existence of civil society, it has also united itself to ensure the fulfilment of the necessary conditions of maintaining civil society, such as providing aid to the poor.

This interpretation, however, is difficult to sustain. First, such an argument presumes that Kant believes that aid to the poor is a necessary condition of the continued existence of civil society. This would certainly have seemed an odd and extravagant claim in late eighteenth-century Europe. Not only does Kant fail to provide the empirical argument required to defend such a claim; Kant makes no explicit claim of this sort in his political writings.

Moreover, the services which Kant lists as necessary for the 'preservation' of the people include not merely aid to the poor, but, in addition, aid to foundling homes and church organizations. If the 'duty' which the sovereign has assumed is, in fact, the duty to act from the postulate of public right, then 'preservation' of the people must mean ensuring the existence of civil society. Odd as it might be to assume that Kant considered aid to the poor essential to maintaining the existence of civil society, it would surely be still more implausible to assume that Kant believed aid to foundling homes or church organizations was necessary for such a purpose.

Perhaps the 'duty' which the sovereign has assumed is not the duty to act from the first juridical postulate, but some other duty. In order to maintain the interpretation that the power to tax and provide services must be grounded in the need to ensure the continued existence of civil society, the duty in question must be essential to the preservation of civil society. Yet what duty of the people, derivable from the first principles of right and essential to the continued existence of civil society, could require the provision of aid to the poor, foundlings, and church organizations?

The minimalist attempt to read this passage as an elaboration of the postulate of public right seems untenable. Rosen (1993) is surely correct when he argues that 'textual support [for the minimalist position] is very largely a mirage' (197).

But if Kant's discussion of aid to the poor is not grounded in the postulate of public right, what grounding can be provided consistent with the metaphysical principles of right? Rosen argues that the 'duty of the people' which the sovereign adopts is the duty of beneficence.

A duty of beneficence binding upon the sovereign, if established, would resolve much of the confusion surrounding the 'aid to the poor' argument, obviating further efforts to unearth a justification grounded in preservation of civil society. Such a duty of beneficence would define a clear basis for the right to assist the poor. This explanation would, of course, ground an *obligation* to assist, not merely a right. But as noted above, Kant's explicit text is ambiguous on precisely this point, and in fact suggests that the sovereign is subject to a duty.

Such a proposal, however, violates Kant's well-defined distinction between right and virtue. The problem here is not that a duty requires the adoption of an end, while political authority can only coerce external acts. As Rosen argues, while the sovereign cannot coerce members of civil society to adopt the end of beneficence, the sovereign may have 'its own duty of benevolence' (191). Since the duty is binding on the sovereign, the sovereign, alone, need adopt the end. Any legislation adopted in connection with this end need only coerce actions consistent with this end.

The problem is rather that the duty of beneficence is imperfect; that is, the duty assigns an end (aiding fellow human beings), but fails to specify necessary and sufficient means. Since the sovereign's obligation to comply with such a duty is paired with the right to utilize the means necessary to achieve the end (see above), the right to act in accordance with a duty of beneficence could significantly expand the sovereign's coercive power without specifying a criterion to limit that power.

Moreover, since the duty is broad, the right/obligation to comply with such a duty could encourage sovereigns to engage in paternalistic meddling. Such a result seems inconsistent with Kant's aim of creating an environment in which individuals can realize their capacity to form and pursue ends.[21]

Rather than introducing a duty of virtue as a highest-order principle of Kant's political theory, I suggest that an alternative interpretation of the 'aid to the poor' passage is available. The passage states that the general will of the people has united itself into society in order to maintain itself perpetually, and that aid to the destitute is in the service of this end. Traditional interpretations have assumed that the passage requires the perpetual maintenance of the mere *empirical existence* of civil society.

Kant's discussion of the right of the state, however, begins with the claim that public right consists of 'the sum of the laws' neces-

---

[21] O'Neill (1989) also argues from the duty of beneficence, or charity, to the social obligation to supply 'some form of welfare state' (232). While acknowledging that charity is an imperfect duty, O'Neill argues that imperfect duties 'often must be allocated [to agents] before needs can be met'. Arguing from the premiss that imperfect obligations are merely obligations 'whose performance is not . . . allocated to specific right-holders' (225), O'Neill argues that 'the allocation of recipients to agents—a process of institutionalization—is indispensable' (231). The 'most appropriate institutionalization' of the obligation of charity '[i]n mass societies' may be 'some form of welfare state' (232). Since O'Neill's argument merely involves the institutionalization of the obligations of agents to each other, her approach appears to avoid granting unacceptably paternalistic authority to the sovereign. O'Neill does not, however, develop an account of the form such an institutionalization should take or the nature of the legislation appropriate to establish the appropriate 'form of welfare state'.

sary 'to bring about a *rightful condition*' (MJ 311, emphasis mine). It is at least plausible, therefore, to suggest that the specific aspect of civil society to be maintained is not its mere empirical existence, but its *rightful condition*. Kant defines 'rightful condition' as 'that relation of men among one another that contains the conditions under which everyone is able to *enjoy* his rights' (MJ 305–6). The necessary *formal* condition for the enjoyment of rights is a constitution[22] (a system of laws embodying public right and establishing a condition of distributive justice).[23] Two substantive conditions, however, must be satisfied in order to establish a constitution: 'it is only in conformity with the conditions of *freedom* and *equality* that [a] people can become a state and enter a civil constitution' (MJ 315, emphasis mine). Freedom and equality are thus necessary conditions for the enjoyment of rights and, therefore, constitutive elements of a rightful condition.

Thus, acting from the postulate of public law appears to require securing conditions in which individuals can enjoy their rights in conformity with the conditions of freedom and equality. Kant defines equality as 'independence from being bound by others to more than one can in turn bind them' (MJ 237).[24] If some individuals are unable to enjoy their rights because they are subject to asymmetric coercion, for example if some individuals are so poor that they lack the ability to maintain freedom of choice in the face

---

[22] 'Public right is therefore a system of laws for a people ... that ... need ... a *constitution*, so that they may enjoy what is laid down as right' (MJ 311).

[23] The formal condition of public right is a system of public justice which determines: (i) 'what conduct is intrinsically *right*'; (ii) 'what way of being in possession is *rightful*'; and (iii) 'what is *laid down as right*' (that is, the specific bearing of 'the given law' in particular cases) (MJ 306). Thus, Kant states that a rightful condition can be characterized as 'a condition of distributive justice' (that is, a condition in which the bearing of the given law upon particular cases is specifiable) (MJ 307). This passage, however, provides merely a formal characterization of a rightful condition. Substantively, a rightful condition requires the promulgation of a 'system of laws', or public right (MJ 311). In order to realize a rightful condition, it will be necessary to determine the content of the system of laws that constitutes public right. This is the subject of 'Public Right' (Part II of the *Rechtslehre*).

[24] It is important to distinguish the 'innate equality' to which we are entitled by virtue of our innate right to freedom (MJ 237) from mere 'political equality', which Kant defines as 'that relation among citizens whereby no-one can put anyone else under a legal obligation without submitting simultaneously to a law which requires that he can himself be put under the same kind of obligation by the other person' (TPP 99). Innate equality is defined more generally as 'independence from being bound by others to more than one can in turn bind them', and includes the authorization 'to do to others anything that does not diminish what is theirs' (MJ 237–8).

of economic incentives offered by the better endowed, the necessary condition of equality has not been satisfied and a rightful
condition does not exist. It is important to note that this claim is
not inconsistent with Kant's notorious assertion that equality as a
subject is 'consistent with the utmost inequality of the mass in the
degree of material possessions' (TP 75). Kant is merely arguing, in
this passage, that the right to equal status as a subject does not itself
require equality of condition. Equality as a subject *does*, however,
require that 'every member of the commonwealth must be entitled
to reach any degree of rank which a subject can earn through his
talent, his industry and his good fortune' (TP 75). Unless individuals are able to pursue their interests free from asymmetric coercion,
this condition will not be satisfied.

Under this interpretation, Kant's claims (MJ 326) can be understood as consistent with his metaphysical account of right. The
sovereign has 'taken over' the duty of the people to act from the
postulate of public right, which requires interventions to preserve
the *rightful condition* of civil society perpetually. Interventions to
eliminate inherently coercive economic conditions are among
those necessary in order to preserve the rightful condition of civil
society.

In addition, unlike the notion of a duty to preserve the 'continued existence' of civil society (through aid to the poor), a duty to
preserve a 'rightful condition' would preserve for the sovereign
a significant (but not excessive) degree of discretion in the choice
of policy. The sovereign would retain the discretion to determine,
through interpretation of the implications of the metaphysical principles of right, what degree of intervention is necessary to preserve
a rightful condition.

Several salient passages in the *Lectures on Ethics* discuss the
possibility that social conditions may be inherently coercive. The
civil order 'is so arranged', Kant argues, 'that we participate in
public and general oppressions'. Acts on behalf of others are,
therefore, 'not . . . an act of kindness and generosity, but . . . a small
return of what we have taken from him in virtue of the general
arrangement' (LE 27: 432). Moreover, 'beneficence to others [is] a
debt we owe' because, 'if men were strictly just, there might be no
poor' (LE 27: 455). These passages appear to adopt explicitly the
view that certain social conditions within the state are inherently
coercive. While extremely suggestive, however, these passages

cannot be viewed as expressing Kant's definitive views. The *Lectures on Ethics* are merely transcriptions, by students, of Kant's lectures. As such, they may misstate or distort Kant's views. In addition, the lecture notes containing these passages were transcribed in 1784, and therefore predate Kant's formulation of his mature views in the critical moral and political works. Nevertheless, the cited passages suggest that Kant was at least receptive to the view that social conditions in the state can be inherently coercive.

While Kant does not, in his mature political works, explicitly argue for a necessary connection between the existence of economic inequality and coercive social conditions, his account of the distinction between active and passive citizens provides a clear representation of such conditions. Certain citizens (e.g. apprentices, house-servants, minors, and women) lack civil personality 'because they have to be under the direction or protection of other individuals' (MJ 315). That is, their economic circumstances make these citizens so dependent upon the will of others that they cannot exercise their wills in an independent fashion.

Kant does not explore the nature of the inequality between active and passive citizens, but it is clear that the relation involves some coercive power held by the active citizens. Thus, for example, Kant asserts that a husband 'possesses' his wife, child, or servant d*e jure*: he possesses them as long as they are alive at some place and at some time (MJ 248). The necessary implication of this assertion is that if a wife or servant run away, the husband or master has the right to pursue them and coercively restore them to their former position.

While the existence of such inequality is not completely inconsistent with the realization of freedom in a just state (MJ 315), inequalities that allow such coercive relations to exist are necessarily hindrances to freedom (even if their existence is not inconsistent with the *existence* of freedom). Kant asserts that dependence is not incompatible with the freedom to be realized in civil society, *as long as* the laws do not prevent passive citizens from 'work[ing] . . . up from this passive condition' (MJ 315). 'Working up' will not be a real option for most passive citizens, however, unless the state intervenes to provide resources and opportunity; and Kant emphatically condemns social conditions that reinforce and preserve inequality and dependence: 'to proceed on the principle that those who are once subjected to these bonds are essentially unfit for freedom and that one is justified in continually removing them farther from it is to usurp the prerogative of Divinity itself, which created men for freedom' (R 176–7 n.).[25]

Thus, social conditions will be inherently coercive, and therefore inconsistent with freedom, if: (i) empirical circumstances hinder the exercise of freedom, so that some individuals may be 'bound by others to more than [the disadvantaged individuals] can in turn bind them' (MJ 237); and (ii) the disadvantaged individuals lack any reasonable hope of 'work[ing] up from this passive condition' (MJ 315). Legislation is necessary: (i) generally, to ensure that empirical circumstances do not hinder the exercise of freedom; and, (ii) more particularly, to ensure that disadvantaged individuals are assured access to the means to 'work up'.

Moreover, Kant's deduction of the concept of intelligible possession suggests that extreme economic inequalities *necessarily* function as hindrances to freedom. Kant argues that an individual cannot act to pursue his ends, and thus realize his internal freedom, unless some form of authority over usable objects is possible: a maxim of 'putting *usable* objects beyond any reasonable possibility of being *used*' is 'contrary to rights', because such a maxim 'would annihilate [the objects] from the practical point of view' (MJ 246). If the individual has no access to any resources which can be to means of action, however, no realization of freedom will be possible. Therefore, individuals who live in extreme poverty are unable to realize any meaningful form of freedom. Although such individuals have surrendered their provisional (natural) rights and entered the civil state, as required by the postulate of public right (MJ 307), the civil state has failed to recognize their rights to freedom within the civil state.[26] In order to redeem the implicit guarantee of the social contract and counteract massive hindrances to freedom, intervention of the sovereign appears necessary to provide for social welfare.

In *Groundwork II*, Kant distinguishes between positive and

---

[25] While Kant argues, notoriously, that passive citizens should be denied suffrage (MJ 315), he nevertheless insists that 'every member of the commonwealth must be entitled to reach any degree of rank which a subject can earn through his talent, his industry and his good fortune' (TP 75).

[26] Kant's description of the original contract describes an exchange in which 'the people give up their external freedom in order to take it back again immediately as members of a commonwealth' (MJ 315–16).

negative concepts of freedom. The negative concept of freedom requires that the will be independent of any determination by alien causes. The positive concept is of the will as a causality subject to laws it prescribes to itself (G 447).

The argument that economic inequality is inherently a hindrance to freedom relies on a similar distinction. An individual who is not outwardly coerced may be said to be negatively free; nothing physically prevents him from pursuing the objects of his will. Such a person may, nevertheless, be de facto constrained as a result of circumstances which are inherently coercive. In the passive citizens example, the economic inequality between master and servant creates a coercive relation between them; the master, through his wealth, is de facto in a position to hinder the freedom of the servants (e.g. to compel them to accept certain terms of employment). The argument that economic conditions can be inherently coercive relies on this notion that the existence of conditions which necessarily compel an individual to make a certain decision can constitute coercion.

If provision for public welfare is a requirement of justice, rather than simply a right of the sovereign, then the disadvantaged can rightfully require the provision of such services. In addition, I suggest that the authority of the sovereign 'to support those members of society who are unable to support themselves' (MJ 326) is implicit in the mutual dependency of citizens that is a defining feature of Kant's account of a rightful civil condition.

Kant stresses that the existence and well-being of all members of the society depends on 'an act of submitting to [the commonwealth's] protection and care' (MJ 326). Since the welfare of all depends on the realization of a rightful civil condition in which the fundamental rights of all citizens may be 'protected', the protection of the rights of any member of society is in the interest of all members of society. In addition, each citizen possesses an equal claim to protection of his rights by virtue of his innate right to freedom. If, as I have argued, the innate right to freedom implies a right to freedom from asymmetric coercion, then provision for the disadvantaged does not further the interest of one segment of society at the expense of another. Rather, the sovereign's provision for the public welfare is in furtherance of the interests of all members of society. Since the rightful condition of civil society united under a general will is a necessary condition for the validity of definitive right-claims to external property (MJ 256), even the property rights of the prosperous depend on the protection of the rights of all members of the society. Thus, no true conflict exists between provisional proprietary right-claims and the just distribution of property as determined by the sovereign as supreme proprietor of the land.

All existing property rights are contingent upon their conformity to the principles of justice. 'If a certain use of freedom is itself a hindrance to freedom . . . [then] coercion that is opposed to this (as a *hindering of a hindrance to freedom*) is consistent with freedom according to universal laws' (MJ 231).[27] If, as I have argued above, persuasive evidence suggests that the existing distribution of property makes inevitable the existence of inherently coercive social relations, the sovereign is both authorized and obligated to define and implement a distributive principle 'in conformity with the conditions of freedom and equality' (MJ 315).

CONCLUSION

I have argued that Kant's account of public right appears to require a substantial theory of social welfare, since such intervention is necessary to eliminate inherently coercive economic conditions. I have also suggested that Kant's account of right is sufficiently determinate to constitute a basis for policy. While I have sketched the outlines of a Kantian theory of social welfare, I have not developed specific policy implications. The account, as presented in this chapter, seems to ground a general principle governing the state's obligation to its members, rather than specifying a basis for positive law. As such, the principle seems consistent with almost any policy which is self-consciously directed to the problem of poverty. Thus, the argument for a Kantian theory of social welfare again faces the content problem: can Kantian theory offer determinate guidance for policy?

The policy implications of Kant's argument for aid to the

---

[27] In addition, Kant writes that 'one is authorized to use coercion against anyone who by his very nature threatens him' (MJ 307). Since agents surrender their rights of coercion to the state, upon entering civil society, the state must possess the right to coerce those agents who, by their very nature, threaten the freedom of other agents within the state.

poor can only be developed once the nature of the constraint which natural law exercises over positive law has been specified. In Chapters 3, 4, and 5, I argue for an account of political judgment capable of defining this relationship.

2

Happiness and Welfare

A traditional interpretation limits Kant's political theory to a variant of classical liberalism, thus undermining the plausibility of a Kantian theory of social welfare. In Chapter 1, I examine and reject three arguments in favour of this traditional interpretation: (i) the claim that Kant's metaphysical principles of right severely constrain the activities of the state; (ii) the claim that Kant's account of right cannot guide the content of positive law; and (iii) the claim that Kant argues for progress through mere coordination.

Historically, however, a fourth argument in favour of the traditional interpretation has been the most influential. This argument is grounded in Kant's explicit rejection of a principle of 'welfare' as a basis for legislation. Many scholars regard this rejection of a welfare principle as decisive in favour of the classic liberal interpretation of Kant's political thought. In this chapter, I will examine the grounding, basis, and extension of Kant's argument.

Kant's vehement rejection of welfare or happiness as a ground for legislation (TP 82–3, CF 183 n., MJ 318) has to many seemed decisive in favour of the traditional interpretation because it appears to *require* a libertarian conception of the state. Kant argues that juridical legislation, like moral legislation, must not be grounded in the realization of a specific end, such as welfare or happiness, since such ends '[do] not have any ruling principle, either for the recipient or for the one who provides it'[1] (CF 183 n.). Principles grounded in welfare or happiness[2] are 'incapable of be-

---

[1] Compare Kant's criticism of grounding ethical principles in the pursuit of an end: 'we cannot know, a priori, . . . whether [achievement of the end] will be associated with pleasure or displeasure' (CPr 21). Ethical principles must, therefore, claim universal validity only 'because of their form and not because of their matter' (CPr 27).

[2] Since Kant directs the same criticisms against principles grounded in (i) welfare and (ii) happiness (MJ 318), I will refer to such principles jointly as hedonic principles.

coming a universal rule', and therefore fail to provide an adequate ground for legislation (CF 183–4 n., TP 82–3). If, as argued in the standard interpretation, these passages have as their target legislation designed to realize material goals such as public welfare, then Kant's account of right does, in fact, impose classic liberal constraints on the power of the sovereign.

Such libertarian interpretations of Kantian political theory have influenced the history of political thought by helping to redefine the classic liberal notion of the state. Humboldt (1969/1852), developing his interpretation of Kant's political thought, argued that state activity must be severely constrained as a necessary condition for the cultivation of autonomy and individuality.[3]

Libertarian interpretations continue to influence the evolution of classic liberal theory. For example, Hayek's influential indictment of the interventionist welfare state is grounded in the following thesis: '[T]he prime public concern must be directed not towards particular known needs but towards the conditions for the preservation of a spontaneous order which enables individuals to provide for their needs'(Hayek 1976: 2). As discussed in Chapter 1, Hayek offers this claim as an interpretation of Kant's assertion that 'juridical laws [must] abstract altogether from our ends, they are essentially negative and limiting principles which merely restrict our exercise of freedom' (Hayek 1976: 43).

While the traditional interpretation appears to reflect a tangible theme in Kant's political writings, this interpretation in fact misconstrues the subject and analytical level of Kant's claims. First, the traditional argument conflates the notion of welfare to which Kant objects with the general notion of social welfare. In fact, Kant specifically limits his objections to a principle of legislation which requires the sovereign to achieve the *happiness* of the subjects (see CF 183 n., TP 80).

---

[3] 'The cultivation of the understanding . . . is generally achieved by [man's] own activity, his own ingenuity, or his own methods of using the discoveries of others. Now, State measures always imply more or less compulsion; and even when this is not the case, they accustom men to look for instruction, guidance, and assistance from without . . . whether it coerces the citizen by some compulsory arrangement . . . or by . . . rewards, and other encouragements attractive to him . . . [the state] will always deviate very far from the best system of instruction. For this unquestionably consists in proposing, as it were, all possible solutions of the problem in question, so that the citizen may select, according to his own judgment, the course which seems to him the most appropriate' (Humboldt 1969/1852: 19).

Second, while Kant argues that a principle of happiness cannot constitute the sole ground of the will's determinations, he does not argue that such a principle can play no part in determining the will. In fact, he explicitly recognizes the legitimate, if limited, role of such a principle (CPr 34).

Third, the traditional interpretation misconstrues the level of generality of Kant's arguments. The passages in which Kant criticizes legislation grounded in a principle of happiness are intended to constrain a possible *system* of legislation, not particular legislative acts. Kant argues that the *relation of the sovereign to his subjects* cannot be grounded in a highest-order principle of legislating to achieve happiness (CF 183 n.). While such an argument may have profound political implications, it does not, in itself, justify a constraint on the considerations which may ground particular acts of legislation.

It is for this reason that Kant believes he is consistent in arguing *against* legislation based on a principle of happiness, but *for* state activity to realize many traditional social welfare goals, such as income maintenance for the poor, subsidized health care, and a national system of public education. Kant does not reject social welfare legislation per se. Rather, he rejects a political principle which assigns to the sovereign the right and responsibility to determine *for* its subjects what the basis of their happiness should be and to secure that basis *for* the subjects, possibly independent of or contrary to their autonomous willing.

While Kant's early *Reflexionen* suggest that he at least considered the possibility that his critique of hedonic principles precluded antipoverty interventions by the state,[4] Kant definitively rejects such an argument in his mature critical writings (MJ 326). Thus, Kant's extended deliberations regarding the implications of a rejecting a principle of happiness led him to consider and *reject* the classic liberal position attributed to him by the traditional interpretation.

Kant's critique of welfare as a legislative principle is best understood as an argument presented within his particular political con-

---

[4] Kant is clearly ambivalent about the antipoverty role of the state at this point in his intellectual development. In *Reflexionen* no. 8000 (xix. 578), Kant argues (Beiser reports) that the state has no responsibility to care for the poor. Yet at approximately the same period, in the *Naturrecht Feyerabend*, Kant argues that the ruler has an ' "imperfect duty" to promote the welfare of his citizens' (see Beiser 1992a: 34).

text. While Kant's case against hedonic principles as a ground for legislation is made in abstract conceptual terms, his critique appears to have been a self-conscious contribution to an ongoing theoretical debate.

For Kant, the arguments in favour of hedonic principles as a ground for legislation would have been associated with a specific political philosophy. Cameralist theorists such as Johann Heinrich Gottlieb von Justi (1717–68) argued that 'the ultimate aim of each and every republic is . . . unquestionably the common happiness' (Justi 1755: 35). In order to secure the common happiness, cameralists argued that the state had a fundamental obligation to maintain high levels of social welfare. This notion of state responsibility for public welfare was paired with advocacy of comprehensive and paternalistic social regulation. In some cases, the regulations took on a repressive character.[5]

Kant was deeply antagonistic to paternalism. The public would almost inevitably enlighten itself, Kant argued, '*if only the public concerned is left in freedom*' (WE 55, emphasis mine). Thus, it seems reasonable to assume that Kant is responding directly to cameralist arguments when he asserts that 'the principle of happiness . . . has ill effects in political right just as in morality'[6] (TP 83).

The cameralists argued that the sovereign must ensure the happiness and moral rectitude of citizens in order to ensure the nation's prosperity. In securing the welfare of the citizens, the sovereign ensured the optimal contribution of each to national prosperity. In this theory, state interventions are in no way related to ensuring the individual agent's capacity for purposes. Such a concern would be at best irrelevant and at worst a hindrance. Thus, cameralism constitutes a statist, paternalistic social philosophy.

Kant encountered cameralist thought most directly in the work of Christian Wolff and his student, Alexander Gottlieb Baumgarten. Wolff was a cameralist, and the 'founder' of the cameralist theory of the welfare state (Dorwart 1971: 17); Baumgarten's

---

[5] For example, Justi proposed to regulate the age from which children could be mourned by their parents (see Dyson 1980: 117–21).

[6] If Kant's political theory is understood as a response to cameralist public welfare arguments, it is not necessary to conclude that Kant opposed the general cameralist notion of state responsibility for public welfare. It is necessary to identify the target of Kant's criticism precisely in order to understand his notion of the state.

ethical and political thought follows Wolff closely. Kant employed
Baumgarten's *Initia philosophiae practicae primae* as the text of an
ethics course which he taught regularly. In his lecture notes, Kant
criticizes both Wolff and Baumgarten for grounding obligation in a
principle of happiness.

The relation of Kant's critique of hedonic principles to the
cameralist political philosophy of the eighteenth-century German
states has been strangely neglected in the secondary literature. Yet
I will argue that the full significance of Kant's argument rejecting
hedonic legislative principles can be understood only in the context
of an investigation of the context in which Kant presented this
argument.

In this chapter, I will examine the role of Kant's critique of
cameralism in his political theory. In section 1, I will examine
Kant's critique of legislation grounded in a principle of happiness.
In section 2, I will argue that Kant's argument is directed specifically against cameralist paternalism.

1. HAPPINESS AND PRACTICAL LEGISLATION

Kant argues that 'no generally valid principle of legislation' can be
grounded in a principle of happiness (TP 80). Moreover, traditional
interpreters have assumed that in referring to 'legislation grounded
in a principle of happiness', Kant referred to legislation whose
benefits are targeted on the poor.

The traditional argument is grounded in four premises: (*a*)
Kant's critique of a principle of happiness is grounded in
the *contingency* of such a principle; (*b*) his objection is categorical;
(*c*) he intends to criticize social welfare legislation, as a category;
and (*d*) he intends his critique to apply directly to particular acts of
legislation. Thus, the traditional interpretation concludes, Kant's
critique specifically condemns social welfare legislation, as an ex-
emplary case of legislation grounded in a contingent principle.

In this section, I will dispute the four premises of the traditional
interpretation and, therefore, reject the conclusion that Kant's critique of legislation grounded in a principle of happiness requires
a categorical condemnation of social welfare legislation. Rather, I
will suggest, Kant's critique is directed against a specific philosophical adversary.

A. *Contingency and Materiality*

Kant's critique of legislation grounded in a principle of happiness is directed against principles of legislation, moral or juridical, which 'place the determining ground of choice in the pleasure or displeasure' to be realized. Such principles 'cannot be valid in the same form for all rational beings', and therefore '[lack] objective necessity' (CPr 21–2). These passages suggest two possible concerns grounding Kant's rejection of hedonic legislative principles: (i) the contingency of the relation of pleasure to any particular empirical outcome; and (ii) the determination of the will by a material, rather than formal, principle.

While these two concerns cannot be entirely separated, since all formal principles for Kant hold non-contingently, it remains important to determine whether one of these concerns has priority in motivating Kant's argument. The answer to this question is particularly relevant in assessing the claims of the traditional interpretation of Kant's views on welfare. In particular, Hayek's interpretation is grounded in the claim that Kant is concerned only with the contingency of the legislation.[7] Unless Kant's concern is in fact grounded in the contingency of the principle, Hayek's theory cannot claim a Kantian pedigree.

The nature of Kant's underlying concern will define: (i) the cases to which Kant's objection applies; and (ii) the burden of persuasion which Kant's argument establishes for principles of legislation. If Kant's primary concern is contingency, then an act of legislation will meet Kant's burden of persuasion if a non-contingent relation can be demonstrated between the objective of the legislation (e.g. education) and the objective of the underlying principle (e.g. happiness). Hayek appears to interpret Kant as imposing this sort of a burden of persuasion. Since, for Hayek, information constraints bar complete knowledge of the consequences of legislative acts, no social intervention can be grounded in a valid principle.

If Kant is concerned only with the contingency of the principle,

---

[7] Hayek's central claim, which he presents as a Kantian criticism of social welfare policy, is that: 'the general welfare at which a government ought to aim cannot consist of the sum of particular satisfactions of the several individuals for the simple reason that neither those nor all the circumstances determining them can be known to government or to anybody else' (Hayek 1976: 2). Thus, Hayek's orientation is consequentialist, and his objection relates to the contingency of a legislative principle grounded in the general welfare.

however, his objection will not count as an objection to principles of happiness which can be shown to hold non-contingently. If, for example: (i) all rational beings desire to maximize their skills; and (ii) the satisfaction of this desire produces pleasure; then (iii) legislation grounded in the principle of producing pleasure by satisfying the desire to realize skills would not be vulnerable to Kant's objection.

Conversely, if Kant's primary concern is with the materiality of the principle, an act of legislation will only meet Kant's burden of persuasion by demonstrating that the legislation is in fact required by a formal principle. This could be shown, for example, if an act of legislation realized an end required by a metaphysical principle of natural law. In this case, Kant's objection would count *only* against legislation grounded merely in a material principle. An act of legislation required by a formal principle would therefore appear to meet Kant's burden of persuasion even if the operation of the legislation is not *necessarily* associated with the realization of an objective required by the underlying principle. For example, if a principle of right requires that the state provide access to education, as a necessary condition of the individual's realization of his capacity for purposiveness, it will not be an objection to the legislation that education does not universally and necessarily result in the realization of this capacity.

Several salient passages suggest that Kant's primary concern is the contingency of the principle. For example, Kant argues that an idea of the good grounded in achieving pleasure and avoiding displeasure is inadequate to ground generally valid principles *because* 'it is impossible to see a priori which idea will be accompanied with pleasure, and which with pain' (CPr 58). Thus, any attempt to derive such principles merely constitutes a contingent prediction of the empirical consequences associated with the realization of an object or end.[8] Similarly, Kant argues that even a principle of universal happiness can never ground laws of the will, since 'the knowledge of [what produces universal happiness] rests on mere data of experience . . . it can give general, but never universal rules' (CPr 36).

Yet these passages are deceptive. Even if rational beings *unanimously* associated pleasure and pain with the same objects, Kant

---

[8] '[I]t would be solely a matter of experience to discern what is immediately good or evil' (CPr 58).

argues, 'the determining ground would still only be subjectively valid and empirical'. A principle grounded in such a unanimous association of pleasure/pain with objects would still lack 'the necessity which is conceived in every law, an objective necessity arising from a priori grounds' (CPr 26). Thus, legislation must embody 'the *formal* principle of the will' (CF 184).[9] Kant's primary concern is clearly the materiality, rather than the contingency, of the principle determining the will.

In fact, while the fundamental metaphysical principle of right derived in the *Rechtslehre* is formal, it is contingent in its relation to consequences in experience. The postulate of practical reason (MJ 246) is a formal principle requiring merely the possibility of rightful external possession as a necessary condition of realization of man's capacity for purposes.[10] But Kant makes no claim that guaranteeing the possibility of rightful possession will necessarily result in the realization of this capacity. Thus, Kant's central argument in the *Rechtslehre* exemplifies his concern with the formality of the principle which determines the will, rather than contingency of the principle's relation to consequences.

The evil which Kant associates with legislation grounded in a material principle is 'heteronomy of choice, or dependence on natural laws' in the determination of the will (CPr 33). If legislation is grounded merely in a principle of pleasure, 'the will does not give itself the law but only directions for a reasonable obedience to pathological laws' (CPr 33). A government established purely on the principle of securing the happiness of its subjects would similarly substitute heteronomous judgments of the head of state for autonomous judgments by its subjects: 'the subjects, as immature children who cannot distinguish what is useful or harmful to themselves, would be obliged to behave *purely passively* [emphasis mine] and to rely upon the judgment of the head of state as to how they *ought* to be happy' (TP 74).

Kant rejects such a relation between sovereign and subjects as inconsistent with the legitimate role of the sovereign as external lawgiver. External legislation is to govern acts, but not incentives. Legislation designed to control incentives is inconsistent with the

---

[9] 'Legislative form, in so far as it is contained in the maxim, is the only thing which can constitute a determining ground of the [free] will' (CPr 30).

[10] The purpose of external right is: 'allowing human beings to exercise their capacity for free choice' (Gregor 1991: 11).

function of a system of external laws: 'allowing human beings to exercise their capacity for free choice' (Gregor 1991: 11).[11] A state in which the judgment of the sovereign is substituted for the judgment of the subjects thus violates the fundamental purpose of the civil condition.

It is because a principle of legislation grounded in happiness violates such a fundamental aspect of the state's legitimate role that Kant's critique is so emphatic. The aspect of the legislation which produces the violation, however, is not the contingency of the principle—as Hayek argues—but the materiality of the principle grounding the will's self-determination.

B. Categorical Character?

Kant appears to reject legislation grounded in a material principle categorically.[12] Yet he acknowledges that a material principle 'can indeed remain' as a factor affecting the content of the will's self-legislation (CPr 34). For example, I may include pursuit of my own happiness in my maxim, although 'only if I include within it the happiness of others'. In such a case, material content (the universal interest in happiness) affects the content of my maxim, but is not its determining ground. The ground here is, rather, the form of universality, which constitutes 'a condition for adding this material to the will' (CPr 34).

Kant's rejection of a categorical criterion for legislation distinguishes his argument from that of Humboldt (1969/1852). Humboldt shares Kant's concern with the effects of paternalism: state interventions are problematic because they 'accustom men to look for guidance and assistance from without' (19). But Humboldt argues from this concern to a direct condemnation of all state interventions: 'State measures always imply more or less compulsion' (19).

Kant's underlying concern is to preserve the active purposive-

[11] Kant grounds his account of civil condition and the state in the necessity of realizing man's innate right to freedom. Members of society possess this innate right 'by virtue of [their] *humanity*' (MJ 237, emphasis mine), which Kant defines as: 'the capacity to set oneself an end' (DV 392). In order to realize the right to freedom as an instantiation of humanity, the state must secure a context in which members are able to realize their faculty to form ends (purposiveness).

[12] '[A] practical precept which presupposes a material and therefore empirical condition must never be reckoned a practical law' (CPr 33–4).

ness of the individual's will. If legislation is grounded in a material principle, Kant believes, the will becomes a passive receptor for legislation. The active quality of the will can be preserved if the will's determinations are *grounded* solely in formal principles. But a formal principle is only instantiable in experience if it is applied to the material of experience. Therefore, legislation must necessarily include references to material goals. A material principle may therefore *contribute* to the content of the will's self-determination (or analogously to the content of external legislation); Kant's limiting condition requires only that the principle *grounding* the determination of the will (analogously, the principle grounding the legislation) must be formal.

Kant's criterion for the legitimacy of legislation, both moral and political, is thus entirely agent-centred. Kant's primary concern is not with the quality of the legislation itself (necessary or contingent), but with the implications which reliance upon such a principle will have for the willing agency (the individual or general will). Grounding the will's legislative determinations in a material principle is inconsistent with the realization of the will's purposive faculty; therefore, Kant rejects material principles as a ground for legislation.

Thus, Kant extends his Copernican shift of perspective to political and moral legislation. In his moral theory, Kant reversed the traditional relation between morality and the source of value, locating moral value in the human will within us, rather than in the providential order outside us.[13] In his account of legislation, Kant continues this reversal of perspective, grounding his criterion of legitimacy not in some notion of the 'good' which the legislation is to realize in the external world, but in the quality of willing (active or passive) implicit in the adoption of such legislation.

Kant argues for this reversal of priority most precisely in the *Critique of Practical Reason*, in his discussion of the 'paradox of method' (CPr 62–3): 'the paradox is that the concept of good and evil is not defined prior to the moral law . . . rather the concept of good and evil must be defined after and by means of the law.' The 'confusions of philosophers concerning the supreme principle of

[13] The Wolffian tradition 'places the source of moral value not in the human will but in the providential order . . . Compared to this tradition, Kant's new ethics are revolutionary. The source of moral value is the moral will inside us, not the providential order outside us' (Beiser 1992a: 31).

morals', Kant argues, resulted because many philosophers (particularly 'the ancients') presupposed the priority of the good to the right. As a result, they 'excluded . . . the possibility of a priori practical laws'; if the good is prior to the right, then the universal determining ground of the will must be the concept of some 'good' object, rather than merely lawful form.

Once the priority of the good was assumed, 'the possibility was already removed of even conceiving a pure practical law' (CPr 63). The error of these philosophers, Kant argues, was in failing to inquire first 'for a law which directly determined the will a priori and only then [seeking] the object suitable to it' (CPr 64). In presuming that the will must be determined by a material principle, Kant suggests, these philosophers neglected the primary question in moral philosophy: the nature of a principle capable of determining the will a priori. Rarely, before Rawls (see Rawls 1971: 30–3, 446–52), had the priority of the right, and its implications for legislation, been presented with such clarity.

C. Kant's Target: Social Welfare Legislation?

Proponents of the traditional interpretation have generally asserted that Kant's rejection of 'considerations of well-being' (CF 184) as a ground of legislation constitutes a direct attack upon the notion of social welfare legislation. In fact, Kant defines precisely the sense of well-being he employs in his critique of hedonic principles of legislation. 'Well-being' is defined, for the purposes of this argument, as 'only a relation to our condition of pleasantness or unpleasantness' (CPr 60). Therefore, when Kant criticizes the role of notions of well-being in legislation, his target is not legislation designed to achieve a certain set of living conditions for its beneficiaries, but rather legislation which is designed to produce the *happiness* of those it affects. Thus Kant stresses that 'happiness . . . cannot be regarded as the end for which a civil constitution was established' (TP 80).[14]

---

[14] Kant returns to this theme almost obsessively throughout section two of 'Theory and Practice': 'No generally valid principle of legislation can be based on happiness . . . happiness alone can never be a suitable principle of legislation' (TP 80). '[S]uch errors arise in part from the usual fallacy of allowing the principle of happiness to influence judgment, where the principle of right is involved' (TP 82–3). 'Under such a *paternal government*, the subjects . . . would be obliged to behave purely passively and to rely on the judgment of the head of state as to how they ought to be happy' (TP 74).

In addition to grounding a critique of Christian Garve's argument that happiness provides the motivation for all practical effort, 'including obedience to the moral law' (see TP 67), Kant's argument constitutes an objection to a possible claim that the sovereign should be bound to observe a duty of charity. First, as discussed in Chapter 1, the imposition of such a duty on the sovereign would invite paternalism, since a wide duty specifies the end, without limiting the degree to which the sovereign should act, nor the range in which action responsive to the duty would be appropriate. But more significantly, Kant's critique suggests, such a duty would in fact be inappropriate as a principle governing the relation of the sovereign to its subjects (CF 183 n.).

Aside from grounding a critique of the specific case of legislating from a principle of benevolence, however, the direct relevance of Kant's critique to social welfare legislation in general is not obvious. While the motive of producing happiness is not unintelligible as a basis for modern social welfare legislation, neither is such a motivation generally the basis for such legislation. Social welfare legislation may be grounded in numerous principles unrelated to the legislation of a basis of happiness to be imposed upon members of the civil condition: (i) social solidarity (reflecting a principled consideration of the obligation of each member of society to his fellow members); (ii) egalitarian refusal to allow arbitrarily unequal endowments to determine life chances; (iii) communitarian identification with a conception of a fair community; (iv) efficiency considerations (the calculation that a people will be more productive if they are healthy and decently nourished); (v) social safety/ crime prevention; or (vi) social control.

Principles (i)–(iii) are formal, and thus clearly not grounded in a principle of happiness. Since principles (iv)–(vi) do not confer any social benefits realized (efficiency, safety, social control) on the direct beneficiary of the policy, they cannot be described as principles which define, and then implement, a principle establishing the basis on which recipients are to be happy. Rather, these three alternatives are neutral with regard to happiness. They could be adopted in the service of a principle of happiness (merely in order to maintain a high standard of living); or in the service of a formal principle (in order to secure the realization or continued existence of a rightful condition).

Moreover, I have argued, Kant's critique does not categorically exclude principles of happiness from contributing to the content of legislation. Rather, Kant's requirement is simply that a principle of happiness must not determine the legislating will. Thus, only in the case of a sovereign (i) explicitly grounding social welfare legislation in a principle of happiness, or (ii) legislating from a duty of beneficence would Kant's critique apply *necessarily* to the resulting social welfare legislation. Most significantly, Kant, who rejects legislation grounded in 'considerations of well-being', nevertheless argues for the right of the sovereign to implement various social welfare interventions, in particular income maintenance[15] (MJ 326), state-funded health services[16] (MJ 367), and a system of public education[17] (CF 189).

Several theorists (Murphy 1970, Aune 1979, Gregor 1995) have argued that the sovereign's right to provide for the poor is grounded in the state's security interests, and that the intervention is justified only to the extent necessary to ensure security. Proponents of this argument apparently assume that Kant intends to proscribe social welfare legislation categorically, but allows an exception just in case the continued existence of the civil condition is contingent upon such legislation. I have argued in Chapter 1, however, that the passage will not support such an interpretation.

Perhaps more significantly, it cannot be consistently maintained that: (i) Kant's prohibition is categorical; and (ii) an exception is justified when necessary to ensure the continued existence of civil society. A categorical requirement is by definition unconditional: such a requirement is by its nature not subject to exception for merely instrumental reasons. Therefore, even security interests essential to the continued existence of the state cannot justify an exception to Kant's prohibition unless the prohibition is not categorical.

[15] '[T]he government is ... authorized to constrain the wealthy to provide the means of sustenance to those who are unable to provide for even their most elementary needs ... [I]t will do this ... by public taxation' (MJ 326).

[16] 'Those institutions for the benefit of the poor, invalids, and the sick that have been set up at the expense of the state (foundations and hospitals) can certainly not be done away with ... [the people are] entitled to the benefits of this foundation'. Kant argues, however, that health care subsidies should replace 'splendid institutions serviced by expensive personnel', since 'it has been found that the poor and the sick ... are cared for better and more economically' through such subsidies (MJ 367).

[17] '[T]he whole mechanism of education ... will be wholly disjointed unless it is designed on the considered plan and intention of the highest authority in the state' (CF 189).

If the prohibition is not categorical, moreover, Kant would need some explicit justification for limiting exceptions to those grounded in national security concerns. Neither Kant nor the commentators offer such a justification. It would seem, therefore, that any intervention whose necessity could be grounded in a formal principle should qualify for a similar exception.

Thus, it seems implausible that Kant intended his critique of hedonic principles as a critique of social welfare legislation in general. In section 2, I will argue that his critique is directed against a particular political philosophy which grounds the relation of the sovereign to the subject in a principle of happiness.

D. Level of Analysis

Finally, Kant does not present his argument as a critique applicable to particular legislation. Rather, he argues against a specific principle designed to structure the relation between the will as morally legislative (*Wille*) and the will as capable of undetermined choice (*Willkür*). In the political context, Kant presents his argument as a critique of principles designed to structure the relation of the general will of all the people, as sovereign, to the will of the people individually, as subjects.

A passage frequently cited as evidence of Kant's rejection of social welfare legislation generally (CF 183 n.) actually demonstrates the inappropriateness of applying Kant's critique to particular legislation. In this passage, Kant asserts that 'welfare does not have any ruling principle'; therefore, 'the rights of men . . . must necessarily come before all considerations of their actual well-being' (CF 183 n.–184 n.). It is tempting to read this passage as an attack on social welfare legislation designed to improve the well-being of recipients. Yet, as we have seen, Kant defines well-being as 'a relation to our condition of pleasantness or unpleasantness' (CPr 60). Thus, this passage from the *Conflict of Faculties* merely extends (from internal to social legislation) the application of Kant's argument that legislation must be grounded in formal, rather than material principles.

Kant begins the passage by observing that no ruler has 'ever dared to say openly . . . that the people owe their happiness only to the *beneficence* of a government which confers it upon them'. The paternalistic principle underlying such a claim is, Kant believes, so obviously unjust that no ruler would dare to declare it. Thus, Kant's target in this passage is a principle which structures civil relations so that 'the supreme power makes laws which are directed towards happiness' (TP 80). A rightful condition requires 'nothing short of a government in which the people are co-legislators' (CF 184 n.). The principle structuring the relation of sovereign to subject must therefore be one in which 'the rights of men, who are expected to obey must necessarily come before all considerations of their actual wellbeing, for they are a sacred institution exalted above all utilitarian values; and no matter how benevolent a government is, it may not tamper with them' (CF 184 n.).

While this passage *does* develop the political significance of Kant's argument, it is not intended to ground a criterion applicable to individual acts of legislation. Rather than criticizing a category of political legislation, Kant is attacking a principle of social organization which defines the state's primary function as the provision of pleasure, or well-being.

Conclusion

The traditional interpretation of Kant's political philosophy maintains that Kant's critique of hedonic principles of legislation grounds a categorical rejection of any form of social welfare legislation. I have argued that: (i) Kant's argument is not categorical; (ii) the argument is not directed against social welfare legislation; and (iii) the argument does not, in fact, constitute a critique of any particular category of legislation. In addition, I argue that Hayek's attempt to link his critique of social welfare legislation to Kant's argument fails, since Hayek grounds his argument in the contingency of the legislation, while Kant grounds his argument in the materiality of the principle grounding the legislation. Humboldt's theory of the limits of state action is also inconsistent with Kant's political theory, since Humboldt insists on a categorical prohibition of state welfare interventions.

2. KANT'S CRITIQUE OF CAMERALISM

Kant directs his critique of hedonic principles of legislation, I have argued, neither at social welfare legislation, nor at any particular category of legislation. Rather, Kant intends to criticize a principle of social organization which defines the state's primary function as the provision of pleasure, or well-being, to its members.

As I suggest in section 1, many formal principles grounded in equality, community, fairness, and solidarity offer viable bases for structuring the relation of the sovereign and its subjects. Kant reserves his criticism, however, for a narrow category of principles, those grounding the relation of sovereign and subject in a particular material principle: the principle of happiness.

Notes preserved in Kant's *Reflexionen*[18] indicate that his critique of hedonic principles was coherently formulated by the 1760s, nearly a decade before Bentham first discussed the 'greatest happiness principle' in *A Fragment on Government* (1776). Since Kant's argument predates Bentham, and the entire school of modern utilitarianism, what political philosophy constitutes the target of his critique?

I will argue that Kant presents his critique in response to the arguments of the cameralists, a highly influential school of political thought in the German principalities of the seventeenth and eighteenth centuries. While conservative in ideology, the cameralists were a moving force in the evolution of the 'continental European tradition [of] the administration as "the state in action"' (Dyson 1980: 118). The cameralist theory of the state's responsibility for the physical and moral well-being of its citizens grounded the influential notion of the state as *Polizeistaat* (police state).

In this section, I will examine: (i) the fit between the cameralist theory of government and the principle of happiness which Kant critiques; (ii) the link which the cameralist focus on a principle of happiness created between (*a*) responsibility for material welfare and (*b*) paternalism; and (iii) Kant's critique of the cameralistic philosophy of Wolff and Baumgarten.

A. Fit

Justi, the most important and prolific member of the school, achieved his greatest influence in the 1750s, as a professor at the

---

[18] In the *Reflexionen*, Beiser reports, Kant argues that 'the sole aim of the state should be to protect the rights of the people rather than to promote their welfare . . . The ruler should be the representative rather than the father of his people, for a father must care for the interests of his children, while citizens are perfectly capable of caring for their own interests' (Beiser 1992a: 34). See *Reflexionen* no. 7452, xix. 451, no. 7854, xix. 535; no. 7749, xix. 506–7.

Collegium Theresianum and a political writer and journalist, and in the 1760s, as a Berlin Berghauptmann in the king's favour. Justi's most influential theoretical works were published in 1755 (*Staatswirthschaft*) and 1756 (*Polizeiwissenschaft*). Thus, Justi's views were prominent in Germany during the period in which Kant formulated his critique.

Moreover, Justi, perhaps uniquely, argues specifically for a relation of the sovereign to his subjects grounded in happiness:

Hence follows the first and universal principle, namely: all the governmental activities of a state must be so ordered that by means of them the happiness of the state may be promoted. (Justi 1756: Section 3)

The substance of all duties of the ruler is accordingly to make his people happy, or to unite the happiness of each several citizen with the general good. All duties of people and subjects may be reduced to the formula, *to promote all ways and means adopted by the ruler for their happiness and obedience, fidelity and diligence.* (Justi 1759: Section 30)[19]

It is hard not to read Kant as responding directly to Justi, when Kant argues that 'happiness alone can never be a suitable principle of legislation . . . If the supreme power makes laws which are primarily directed towards happiness . . . this cannot be regarded as the end for which a civil constitution was established' (TP 80).

Beiser (1992a) notes that the unifying feature of German conservatism, as it re-emerged in the 1790s, was 'allegiance to the old paternalism . . . that the purpose of the state is to promote the welfare, religion and morality of its subjects' (282). Thus, Neiman (1994) suggests that some elements of Kant's late polemics against paternalism may have been addressed to the emerging conservative movement. Yet Kant's critique was formulated in the 1760s, decades before the conservative resurgence of the 1790s.

Perhaps more significantly, only the cameralists united paternalism with an explicit theory of the state organized around a principle of happiness. Thus, while Kant may have addressed his later critiques of paternalism in part to the new conservatives of that era, he reserved his sharpest and most theoretically powerful criticism for cameralism, which he may have recognized as grounding the new conservatism.

While Kant's political analysis is essentially abstract and conceptual, his arguments are nevertheless informed by contemporary

---

[19] In these two passages, I have followed the translations in Small (1909: 310, 413).

political thought and controversy. Kant's critique of a legislative principle of happiness represents a rejection of a well-defined notion in eighteenth-century German political theory.

But what, precisely, does Kant reject? Cameralist thought represents a synthesis of medieval and Roman political concepts (see Dorwart 1971: 1–22). From medieval theory, this synthesis retains two elements: (i) the absolute authority of the individual monarch; and (ii) the definition of welfare in terms of the moral character of the individual (welfare as 'the private conduct of the governed') characteristic of the 'Christian-feudal heritage' (Dorwart 1971: 6).[20]

The new synthesis fundamentally reorients medieval theory, however, in introducing the Roman notion of collective welfare. Medieval concern for the general good, influenced by the Christian notion of welfare-as-virtue and by the grounding of the feudal state in 'personal rather than public or civic relations', focused on the welfare of the individual (see Dorwart 1971: 1–22). Cameralism, while retaining the medieval concern with virtue and happiness, transferred this concern to the collective level. Cameralism also retains the medieval notion of the absolute personal power of the sovereign. In assigning to the absolute sovereign the authority to promote virtue by regulating private conduct, therefore, cameralism appears to authorize unrestricted regulation of individual affairs in the name of collective welfare. Thus cameralism: (i) gives priority to collective happiness rather than individual independence; (ii) assigns absolute authority to the sovereign at the expense of individual rights; and (iii) retains the sovereign's medieval authority to regulate private conduct paternalistically to ensure individual virtue.

Kant's political theory preserves the medieval focus on the individual, although within the context of a theory oriented by the Enlightenment focus on rights, rather than virtue. Thus, Kant rejects the cameralistic shift of perspective from individual to collective. Moreover, Kant shares the Enlightenment view that political legitimacy derives from consent; thus, individuals possess rights which are prior in status to the state's authority. Kant therefore rejects the cameralistic assignment of absolute priority to the

---

[20] 'This explains why so large a segment of the welfare regulation was sumptuary in nature' (Dorwart 1971: 6).

power and interests of the sovereign. Finally, Kant rejects the notion that external legislation can or should regulate internal incentives, and thus rejects the cameralistic legitimation of paternalistic regulation.

Thus, Kant's critique of cameralism does not appear to bear *necessarily* on legislation designed to address the individual's material welfare. Legislation providing for material welfare *and* grounded in a principle of happiness is subject to Kant's critique. Legislation providing for material welfare, *but* grounded in a formal principle (for example, realizing a requirement of a principle of natural law) should, however, not be similarly objectionable. It is for this reason that Kant can argue consistently: (i) against a legislative principle of happiness; but (ii) in favour of specific legislation providing for material welfare.

B. Happiness, Material Welfare, and Paternalism

Cameralism constituted an oddly hybrid form of political theory, presenting itself as both political and economic theory, and containing elements of both liberal and conservative thought. The cameralists were perhaps the earliest political philosophers to argue for the state's responsibility to ensure a minimal level of well-being to its citizens. As the previous section suggests, however, cameralism also rationalized much paternalistic regulation of the lives of its citizens.

Cameralism emerged from medieval and early Renaissance political theory which was informed with the content of church teachings concerning individual responsibility: 'The [feudal] prince's concern for the utilitarian and moral welfare of his dependents was part of his patrimonial jurisdiction' (Dorwart 1971: 7). No trace is present, in feudal politics or theory, of the Roman notion of *salus populi*, the collective material welfare of all members of the society.

As Roman traditions were reintroduced in the early Renaissance, the notion of the sovereign's responsibility to his subjects underwent a subtle shift. The notion of duty to ensure welfare became a concern for material well-being. Moreover, the focus shifted from the individual to the collectivity (see Dorwart 1971: 6). The sovereign was to ensure the well-being of the whole nation *by* ensuring the well-being of its collective members. The combination of (i) the medieval focus on the sovereign's autocratic powers; (ii) the expansive Roman notion of collective welfare; and (iii) the medieval inclusion of moral condition among politically addressed aspects of welfare, ensured that the late medieval notion of the sovereign's duty to ensure well-being justified and encouraged paternalistic regulation on a significant scale.

Early cameralists balanced tendencies towards paternalism with respect for the value of the impartial rule of law. In the sixteenth century, Melchior von Osse (1506–56), one of the earliest cameralist philosophers, emphasized both points. In a passage which Kant might have found sympathetic, Osse argues eloquently for the rule of law:

Government over men is such a high, precious and wonderful thing that no human being . . . is to be intrusted with exercising it according to his own will, caprice and opinion . . . (man) must be governed by something higher and more excellent than man himself, if government is to be stable . . . therefore almighty God, out of special grace to human kind, has ordained the means of common written law . . . in order that [magistrates and judges] may govern others and render justice without any hindrance of inordinate inclinations and affections. (Osse 1717/1556: 33)

Osse's admiration for the impartial rule of law might appear consistent with a theory of limited government and state restraint. Osse argues, instead, for activist and paternalist government. The ruler should intervene to maintain the people 'in good prosperous circumstances, which occurs when the people live virtuously . . . and everything through which such promotion of things useful to the community is hindered [should be] either averted or prevented' (Osse 1717/1556: 30).

Osse may fail to recognize any tension between the impartial rule of law and activist, paternalistic intervention because his purpose is merely to sketch the foundations of 'good, godly righteous government, judiciary and *Polizei*' (Osse 1717/1556: 33). As Small (1909: 32) notes, Osse's argument does not represent a systematic exposition of the themes of cameralism, but rather 'a picture of undifferentiated confusion, with which to compare the highly articulated system of two centuries later'. Nevertheless, Osse's articulation of the relation between activism, paternalism, and prosperity established a precedent followed, to some extent, by the succeeding cameralists.

The theme of legalism, however, rapidly declined in importance as the later cameralists focused more closely on the objective of ensuring the prosperity of the state. Georg Obrecht (1547–1612), writing in 1609, articulated this shift in emphasis: prosperity was to be achieved through the 'improvement of the physical, mental, and moral life conditions of all the people' (Small 1909: 46).

The work of Ludwig von Seckendorff (1626–92), perhaps the most prominent cameralist before Justi, exemplified the union of welfarism in pursuit of prosperity which characterizes cameralist thought: 'Princely government [is] . . . enforced and exercised . . . for the maintenance and promotion of the common profit and welfare' (Seckendorff 1675: 52). Order and law remain goals of the state, but these goals, themselves, are of value because they promote 'the welfare and general good of the fatherland' (Seckendorff 1675: 203).[21]

Seckendorff's careful examination of the notion of commitment to the general welfare also, however, developed a significant welfarist commitment which would thereafter characterize cameralistic thought. Seckendorff articulates the notion of state responsibility for the subject's material welfare as an implication of the commitment to the general welfare: 'no subject shall lack means for the necessaries of life except through his own fault' (Seckendorff 1675: 204).

Johann Heinrich Gottlob von Justi (1717–68) produced the final synthesis and transformation of cameralism which influenced the social science of Kant's generation. Justi, like his predecessors, emphasized the pursuit of prosperity through the improvement of the material welfare of the citizens. Justi, however, introduced a new refinement: the principle of happiness. All interventions of the ruler and improvements in the material welfare of the people and the general prosperity of the nation were to be understood as embodying the realization of the union of the welfare of the ruler and the happiness of the subjects. The pursuit of these related goals, Justi argues, 'can never be separated' (Justi 1755: 53).

Thus, Justi defines the relation of the sovereign and subjects as structured by a principle of happiness. It is just such a principle structuring the relation of sovereign and subjects which Kant rejects in his critique of a legislative principle of happiness. More-

---

[21] Cited in Dorwart (1971: 5).

over, Justi's analysis of the implications of the principle of happiness manifests precisely the tendency towards paternalism which Kant deplored: 'The monarch must make use of means and measure through which . . . his subjects may be *made* happy . . . The subjects must facilitate these measures by their obedience and diligence' (Justi 1755: 53).

Moreover, cameralism remained essentially a philosophy of state power. In all cases, the maintenance and extension of state power was assigned priority over other values.[22] The philosophy's origins in a period of absolutism 'gave the conception of *Polizeistaat* a repressive character'. Thus, for example, Justi recommended regulating the age 'from which deceased children could be mourned by their parents' (Dyson 1980: 119).

Nevertheless, cameralism included in its paternalism a theory of the state's responsibility for social welfare. The influence of cameralistic theory can be seen, for example, in Bismarck's first social insurance proposal. The state, Bismarck argued, 'is not only an institution of necessity, but one of welfare' (Dyson 1980: 120).

Cameralistic welfare interventions, however, are generally conceived as to some degree imposed by the sovereign upon the citizens. The sovereign designs a policy to 'make' the people happy, and the people have a duty of 'obedience and diligence' in implementing the policy (Justi 1756: 53). In its combination of paternalistic regulation and moral interventionism, cameralism thus typifies the relation of sovereign to subject which Kant attacks in his critique of the legislative principle of happiness.

C. Kant and Cameralist Thought

Kant encountered cameralist theory most directly in the work of Christian Wolff and his student, Alexander Gottlieb Baumgarten. Kant's early studies were heavily influenced by Wolff's teachings. Kant's studies at the Friederichskollegium (1732–40) were supervised by Albert Schutz, an important student of Wolff; while, at the Albertina University of Königsberg (1740–6), Kant studied philosophy, theology, classical Latin literature, mathematics, and the natural sciences with Martin Knudsen, another student of Wolff (Hoffe 1994: 9–10).

---

[22] 'The state had to be all-powerful since, in the last resort, its welfare must transcend the individual and particular interests of individuals within the state' (Chapman 1970: 17).

During the period of Kant's education and early academic career, Wolff's philosophy 'had a profound symbolic significance ... represent[ing] the very vanguard of the *Aufklärung*' (Beiser 1992b: 29). Following Leibniz, Wolff argued for a rigorously deductive philosophical method analogous to the scientific methods of inquiry employed by Descartes and Newton. Wolff's efforts were resisted by Pietists such as A. C. Crusius, who rejected the notion that philosophers can 'construct concepts according to definitions, like the mathematician' (Beiser 1992b: 29). Strenuous debate between the Wolffians and the Pietists persisted during Kant's early academic career, and Kant himself contributed to the debate in his submission to the prize competition set by the Academy of Sciences in Berlin in 1761.

Kant's engagement with Wolffian metaphysics is familiar territory. Less familiar is the fact that Wolff was a cameralist, and, in particular, 'the founder ... of the "cameralistic welfare state"' (Dorwart 1971: 17). This aspect of Wolff's work was extraordinarily influential, forming 'the philosophical basis on which the civil laws of the Prussian state were codified in 1794', and thus influencing 'the theory and actuality of the welfare state under Frederick the Great' (Dorwart 1971: 18).

Wolff's cameralism was eclectic, combining the traditional cameralist emphasis on promoting happiness with Leibnizian perfectionism. Wolff argued that all obligation, moral or political, derived from the obligation to seek perfection. Pleasure or happiness, Wolff argued, is 'but a confused awareness of an increase in perfection' (Schneewind 1997: p. xx). Obligation is thus intimately connected with the promotion of happiness. Obligatory actions are those actions that will bring about so much happiness 'that we cannot bring ourselves to do anything else' (Schneewind 1998: p. xxi). Moreover, '[a]s we come to be more perfect, we also come to ... take more and more pleasure in [the happiness of others]' (Schneewind 1997: p. xx). Thus, for Wolff, the cameralist principle of promoting happiness is a corollary of perfectionism.

Kant's academic duties led him to engage frequently with Wolff's ethical and political thought. In his course on ethics, which he taught at the Albertina University at Königsberg approximately thirty times[23] between 1762 and 1793, Kant employed as his text a

---

[23] 'There is some uncertainty because occasionally lectures were announced but not given' (Schneewind 1997: p. xxv n.). Schneewind (1997), on the basis of available records, states that Kant taught ethics 'nearly thirty times' (xiii).

work by Wolff's student Baumgarten: *Initia philosophiae practicae primae*. Baumgarten, while an original philosopher of aesthetics, followed Wolff literally in his ethical and political thought. The *Initia philosophiae practicae primae* is thus merely an exegesis of Wolff's ethical, political, jurisprudential, and economic thought.

Kant's critique of Wolff's and Baumgarten's thought is preserved in the notes of students who attended Kant's ethics course between 1762 and 1793. Since the subject of Kant's course was ethics, rather than right, Kant's comments focus on the adequacy of Baumgarten's account of obligation, rather than on the nature of the principle appropriate to structure the relation between sovereign and subjects. Nevertheless, Kant's comments clearly indicate the nature and limited range of the concerns motivating his critique of hedonic principles of legislation. In particular, the lectures supplement the later versions of the critique of hedonic principles by defining more precisely the nature of the 'principle of happiness' that, Kant argues, 'can never be a suitable principle of legislation' (TP 80).

Wolff and Baumgarten, Kant asserts, argue that moral duty to oneself 'consists in promoting one's own happiness' (LE xxvii. 340). Such an account of moral duty is unacceptable, Kant argues, because '[h]appiness is no ground, no *principium*, of morality' (LE xxvii. 304). In fact, a '*principle of happiness*' is 'totally adverse to morality' (LE xxix. 623, emphasis mine). In arguing that moral perfection requires 'us to . . . promote our own happiness' (LE xxvii. 340), Wolff reduces moral perfection to 'a means to ends grounded in desire and aversion' (LE xxvii. 16). As such, Wolff confuses moral and practical perfection. Because Baumgarten follows Wolff's account of moral duty, '[t]his distinction [between moral and practical perfection] is bungled by Baumgarten throughout his entire book' (LE xxvii. 16). Moral duty cannot be grounded in a principle merely requiring the satisfaction of the desire for pleasure. Rather, such duty is generated when the will is 'determin[ed] . . . by pure motivating grounds of reason' (LE xxix. 598).

Since Kant argues that the ground of moral duty must be self-legislation, his claim that a principle of happiness cannot be the determining ground of duty is equivalent to the claim that a principle of happiness cannot be a suitable ground for legislation. Only 'pure motivating grounds of reason' constitute a suitable ground for legislation. Since pure grounds of reason contain no reference to material ends, and are thus by definition formal rather than

material, Kant is claiming that only a formal principle may constitute such a suitable ground.

Kant's fundamental criticism of Wolff and Baumgarten is, therefore, that they attempt to ground legislation in a material, rather
than formal, principle. Yet this is precisely the core of Kant's
critique of hedonic principles of legislation in the *Critique of Practical Reason*, the *Rechtslehre*, and the *Conflict of the Faculties*. Thus,
in his critique of cameralist ethical and political thought, predating
the *Critique of Practical Reason*, the *Rechtslehre* and the *Conflict of
the Faculties* by four, thirteen, and fourteen years, respectively,[24]
Kant anticipates the concerns and structure of his critique of
hedonic principles of legislation. Moreover, the specific nature of
the 'principle of *happiness*' that Kant criticizes is quite clear. In
grounding duty in a principle of happiness, Kant argues, Wolff and
Baumgarten argue for 'a general rule directing us to satisfy all our
inclinations and promote our own happiness' as the highest principle of morality (LE xxvii. 340).

CONCLUSION

I have argued that Kant's critique of hedonic principles is: (i)
not categorical; (ii) not directed against social welfare legislation;
and (iii) not intended to establish a criterion for individual acts of
legislation. Rather, Kant intends to criticize the notion that a principle of happiness might structure the relations of the sovereign
and subjects, generally. In addition, I have argued that Kant objects
to the materiality of such a principle, not to its contingency.

In the course of the analysis, I have suggested that the interpretations of Kant's critique of hedonic principles offered by Hayek
and Humboldt both diverge from Kant's actual argument. Hayek's
interpretation is not fully reflective of Kant's perspective because
Hayek understands Kant to object to the contingency of hedonic
principles, while I have argued that Kant is concerned primarily
with the material nature of the principle. Humboldt fails to produce
an interpretation faithful to Kant because he claims that the danger
of paternalism, implicit in material principles of legislation, justifies

---

[24] In the Collins notes dating from 1784, Kant articulates clearly the argument
anticipating the critique of hedonic principles. Even the Herder notes dating from
1762, however, clearly set forth the main elements of the argument.

a categorical exclusion of such principles; Kant, I have suggested, argues only for a non-categorical exclusion.

More generally, I believe both theorists diverge from Kant because they adopt and then distort a central Kantian theme. It is central to Kant's argument that policy and legislation must not be determined merely by consideration of the pleasure or displeasure to be caused by the consequences. Rather, the will must be determined by a formal principle.

Humboldt and Hayek, however, in their determination to bar consequentialism from legislative judgment, inflate Kant's concerns with contingency and paternalism into categorical principles. As I have argued, however, Kant's critique of hedonic principles appears to have been intended as a contribution to a contemporary dispute. His criticisms were directed towards a particular political philosophy which exemplified the paternalism, grounded in a contingent material principle of legislation, which Kant deplored. Kant fails to disaggregate his arguments and establish the priority of his concerns because he is engaging in controversy, rather than systematic philosophy.

I have argued, however, that a careful reading of Kant's arguments does not support the traditional interpretation of Kant's critique of hedonic principles. Kant does not wish to eliminate the possibility of welfare legislation, but rather to limit the set of principles which may legitimately ground such legislation. Rather than offering an endorsement of right as merely a system of external duties, Kant argues that the moral will must rise '*beyond* mere obedience to formal laws and [create] as its own object the highest good' (TP 65 n.). Kant's remaining task is to define the role of this notion of the highest good in determining the content of political life.

3

Teleology, Rational Faith,
and Context Dependence

I F a civil society is to realize a rightful condition, I have argued, the metaphysical principles of natural law must be embodied in positive legislation. Thus, the principles of natural law must influence and constrain the content of positive legislation in a manner generating specifiable implications for policy.

In order to specify these implications, Kant must shift the perspective of his analysis. In the *Rechtslehre*, Kant limits his inquiry to a metaphysical question with limited normative significance for positive legislation: given the concept of right and the notion of humans as free, but 'radically evil',[1] what principles ground the legitimacy of positive law? Thus, Kant presents his account as 'a system of a priori knowledge from concepts alone' (MJ 216). This characterization reflects Kant's view that legislation, both moral and juridical, must be grounded in principles which exclude all consideration of material ends. Rather, legislation must embody 'the *formal* principle of [the] will' (CF 184 n). Kant's approach appears to preclude not merely consequentialism, but the teleological notion that an account of right for intentional agents should reflect their goal-directed nature. This apparent rejection of the relevance of material ends to legislative willing has grounded the objection that Kantian right is implausibly rigoristic (Williams 1985: 62 ff.)

Yet remarkably, in light of Kant's insistence that the ground of legislation must be completely formal, a significant strand of Kant's account of political right investigates the role of teleological judgment in determining what end the norms, laws, and institutions of a rightful civil condition should serve. In specifying the purpose which

---

[1] Radical evil consists in 'mak[ing] the incentive of self-love and its inclinations the condition of obedience to the moral law' (R 32).

a civil condition is to realize, teleological judgment makes possible the specification of an idealized notion of the civil condition against which social practices in experience can be evaluated.[2] This ideal-ized notion of the highest political good serves as a criterion for the evaluation of existing institutions: the rule for a rightful civil con-dition must be derived, 'as a norm for others, . . . from the ideal of a rightful association of men under public laws'[3] (MJ 355). Moreover, I will argue, this political ideal derives from the reflective specification of the metaphysical principles of natural law.

Kant's modification of his account of judgment to introduce a faculty (reflective judgment) that 'ascend[s] from the particular in nature to the universal' (CJ 180) constitutes one of several signifi-cant revisions, in the *Third Critique*, of the account of cognition developed in the *First Critique*. Why, one might ask, does Kant revise his fundamental assumptions in his third and final critique? Kant offers an explicit rationale. '[A]n immense gulf is fixed', Kant asserts, between the domains of theoretical and practical legislation (CJ 175–6). Yet practical legislation *is* to influence relations in experience: 'the concept of freedom is to actualize in the world of sense the purpose enjoined by its laws' (CJ 176). Thus, 'there must after all be a basis *uniting* the supersensible that underlies nature and the supersensible that the concept of freedom contains prac-tically' (CJ 176). Kant's intense pursuit of this basis leads him to reassess arguments developed in earlier works of critical philoso-phy. In particular, Kant revises his accounts of: (i) the status of teleology as a principle of judgment; (ii) the nature and status of the highest good; and (iii) the status of systematicity as a necessary condition of scientific inquiry.

While undermining the objections from emptiness and rigorism, Kant's incorporation of teleology as a central strand in his account of right has served to ground a second set of objections to Kantian right. It has been objected that Kant's teleological analysis: (i) argues improperly from an account of indeterminate and unspec-ifiable objective moral ends to determinate political claims; (ii) fails to ground a plausible method for the specification of teleological

---

[2] '[P]erpetual peace and the kind of constitution that seems most conducive to it' constitute the 'highest political good', 'the entire final end of the Doctrine of Right within the limits of reason alone' (MJ 354–5).

[3] 'What is incumbent upon us as a duty is . . . to act in conformity with the Idea of [perpetual peace]' (MJ 354).

ends of politics; (iii) argues in a manner generally inconsistent with the premisses of Kant's critique of hedonic principles of legislation; and (iv) extends the moral teleology of the *Critique of Practical Reason* in an inconsistent and speculative manner.

In this chapter I will evaluate Kant's account of political teleology in light of these objections and argue that Kantian political teleology specifies the normative implications of the metaphysical principles of natural law for positive law. In section 1, I will examine the grounding of Kant's teleology in his account of objective ends. In section 2, I will examine the problem of reflective specification of political ends: does Kant's account of teleology offer adequate resources to ground the specification of determinate political ends? In section 3, I will argue that Kant's political teleology remains consistent with his moral theory. In section 4, I will argue that Kant's political employment of teleology is practical, and thus entirely distinct from the merely cognitive employment of teleology in Kant's philosophies of history and religion.

1. TELEOLOGY AND OBJECTIVE ENDS

Kant's moral teleology derives from his account of objective ends. The status of Kant's account of objective ends in the *Groundwork* and the *Doctrine of Virtue* is ideal rather than practical, however, rendering the political significance of objective ends obscure. In this section, I will examine Kant's argument for the practical relevance of objective ends.

Kant argues that in striving to determine a systematically unified set of (obligatory) moral maxims, practical reason simultaneously determines a system of moral ends (G 433, see CPr 108). Kant claims that the ideal form of such a system, the highest good, would be characterized by a synthetic (real, rather than analytic) connection of virtue and proportionate happiness (CPr 111).

This claim is grounded in the premiss that the understanding necessarily presents purposive organization as analogous to intentional purposiveness (CJ 407–8). Since morality constitutes a particular form of purposiveness, we necessarily present the moral domain to ourselves as though it were constituted intentionally by some rational being. We could not imagine that such a being would choose as the highest good a state in which individuals were perfectly virtuous but miserable (see CPr 110–11). *Ceteris paribus*, a state of affairs in which virtuous rational beings achieve happiness proportionate to their moral merit would always constitute a higher good than a similar state of affairs in which the virtuous do not achieve proportionate happiness. However, since the highest good cannot be 'the determining ground' of the moral will (CPr 109), we cannot further the realization of the highest good by acting to promote some consequence, such as happiness. Therefore, the 'happiness in exact proportion to morality' which is to characterize the highest good (CPr 110) must be entirely the product of morally motivated action: the moral action must cause the happiness.

Since the highest good constitutes the union of all *obligatory* ends, all moral agents are committed to the 'realization *or* promotion' of this end (CPr 109, emphasis mine).[4] While the realization of the highest good is the necessary object of a moral will, such a realization requires a complete rationality of which no existing agent is capable. Therefore, the real object of the will is not the achievement of such an end, but 'endless progress' towards that goal. The 'moral destiny' of mankind is 'an infinite progress towards complete fitness to the moral law' (CPr 122–3).

While the agent is committed to 'do all in [his] power' to further the highest good, this requirement apparently fails to ground determinate practical obligations: the agent can further this goal only by acting from respect for the moral law, per se. The goal of furthering the highest good appears to offer no new input which might affect the agent's practical deliberations: in choosing her maxim of action, the agent still chooses solely on the basis of pure practical reason (see Beck 1960: 244). Thus, the teleological argument in Kant's moral theory tells us that we should understand our rational maxims as necessarily connected to a systematic unity of ends, but offers no positive account of the significance of that relation for practical deliberation.

This ambiguity is reflected in Kant's characterization of the highest good as an *ideal* of reason (A810/B838). An ideal constitutes an archetype which provides a 'standard for our actions . . . enabling

---

[4] The status of moral teleology is ambiguous in this passage. The passage refers to the 'promotion' or 'realization' of the highest good. Yet these two terms have different implications. The agent could contribute to the 'realization' of the highest good simply by acting from the moral law. 'Promotion' of the highest good, however, seems to imply activity directed towards a specific goal.

[reason] to estimate and to measure the degree and the defects of the incomplete'. Reason aims at 'complete determination' of the objects which it conceives as ideals. Such a complete determination is conceivable under the principle of determinability: any object can, in principle, be determined, either affirmatively or negatively, against the sum total of all disjunctive predicates (A572/B600). Therefore, any object can, in theory, be fully determined if it can be compared to 'the sum of all possible predicates' (A573/B601).

Nevertheless, Kant initially argues that an ideal cannot be exemplified as a concrete 'individual' entity. Such a complete determination is 'a concept which can never be exhibited *in concreto* (A573/B601). In fact, there is something 'absurd, and far from edifying, in such an attempt' (A569–70/B597–8).

Thus, the moral argument suggests that no determinate account of the highest good can be achieved. I will argue that Kant only conceives of a political role for the principle of teleology after he has developed a methodology for rendering determinate the teleological ends implicit in his moral argument.

2. SPECIFICATION OF POLITICAL ENDS

Kant's teleological argument is grounded in the claim that an intrinsic connection exists between one's choice of a maxim of action and the choice of an end. Since human activity is necessarily 'purposive', or directed towards the achievement of certain ends (G 427), the free decision to ground one's act in a maxim is simultaneously the choice of an end (DV 385, 389).

Kant argues that some ends must also be duties. That is: (i) the adoption of a particular maxim can be a duty;[5] and (ii) each obligatory maxim has a *unique* end associated with it. Kant believes he has established the first claim in the *Critique of Practical Reason*. If the first claim is accepted, and if Kant is correct to assume that all maxims chosen through practical deliberation are necessarily linked to ends, then the second claim follows logically. Therefore, the notion of objective ends does appear to follow necessarily from Kant's premisses.

While Kant does not specify a method for identifying obligatory

---

[5] This is, of course, the central claim of his moral theory.

ends, such a method can be derived from the contradiction in the will test, which evaluates the permissibility of maxims of ends. Obligatory ends can be identified by refining the application of this test to maxims with permissible ends. If the negation of a permissible maxim cannot be universalized, the maxim and the end associated with the maxim are obligatory. For example, the maxim 'to assist the less fortunate' is permissible. Since the negation of this maxim is not permissible (G 423), the maxim, along with any ends necessarily associated with it, is obligatory.

Kant's teleological argument, however, appears vulnerable to two objections relating to the problem of specification. First, it has been argued that Kant's account of objective ends cannot ground a specific conception of a political end in experience. Second, even if a specification is theoretically possible, such a specification must be radically indeterminate because of the problem of context dependency.

In this section I will evaluate objections to Kant's account of teleology grounded in the problems of (i) specification and (ii) context dependency. Finally, I will evaluate the resources available to address these objections in Kant's account of reflective judgment.

A. Determinacy

The conflict in the will procedure identifies objective ends in the case that (i) the agent's maxim is permissible; and (ii) the negation of this maxim cannot be universalized. This procedure may, however, fail to identify a *unique* obligatory end. In fact, as Allison (1994) argues, the procedure fails to take account of Kant's own distinction between ends as limiting conditions and positive ends.[6]

The problem, Allison argues, is that a unique objective end is not

---

[6] Kant uses the term 'end' in two different senses (see Gregor 1963: 83–4). Used in the first sense, the term refers to the object (goal) which determines the will to action. Such goals are not limited to objects or states of affairs; the *Doctrine of Virtue* focuses on ends defined as dispositions, specifically dispositions to act from moral motivation (DV 383–4). For example, in acting from a maxim to donate to charity, one would be grounding one's maxim in the end of acting beneficently. Used in the second sense, the term refers to 'a limiting condition on our actions'; the notion of autonomy operates as such a limiting condition since the thought of the autonomy of others prevents us from treating them as mere means (see Gregor 1963: 84).

specifiable in many cases in which the negation of a permissible maxim, such as the maxim of beneficence, cannot be universalized. Allison suggests two alternative ways of rejecting a maxim of non-beneficence: adopt a maxim of beneficence; or acknowledge an onerous requirement to act beneficently. Moreover, Allison does not seem to have exhausted the plausible alternatives. For example, one could adopt a maxim to act beneficently, but only on behalf of: (i) members of a specific disadvantaged class; (ii) members of one's own community; or (iii) members of disadvantaged communities. Thus, the determination that a maxim of omission is impermissible does not necessarily entail the adoption of one unique maxim of commission.

This objection is directed to the possibility of identifying objective ends, not their logical necessity. Nevertheless, if objective ends are not identifiable, their theoretical existence will not contribute to ethical or political theory.

Kant avoids this kind of indeterminacy, however, by providing an 'auxiliary [synthetic] principle . . . for the derivation of positive duties' (Allison 1993: 21). This principle requires that the agent 'act in accordance with a maxim of *ends* that it can be a universal law for everyone to have' (DV 395). In requiring that the agent adopt a maxim of ends, the principle rules out the 'onerous requirement to act beneficently' as an alternative to adopting a maxim of acting beneficently: one cannot adopt 'acting beneficently' as an end, and simultaneously view such action as onerous. Similarly, one cannot adopt beneficence as an end and simultaneously will that all agents aid *only* a particular subcategory of the needy. In requiring that the maxim satisfy a universalization requirement, the principle rules out the 'limited maxim to act beneficently' as an alternative.

B. Context Dependence

While this synthetic principle eliminates indeterminacy under a given set of facts, indeterminacy may remain a problem in the context of dynamically changing states of affairs. Thus, context dependence remains a possible objection. For example, Kant argues that the end of cultivating one's capacities, particularly those of the understanding, is objective (DV 386–7). Nevertheless in certain contexts, the agent may determine that a maxim of not cultivating his capacities is morally required. For example, individual *A* lives in a developing country in which a minimum level of social welfare can be maintained only if all educated citizens devote themselves to the supervision and maintenance of emerging industries. Such work is intellectually unchallenging and engages none but the most primitive of the individual's talents. Thus, all efforts to develop his intellectual capacities depress *A*, because they impress upon him the stultifying nature of his obligatory work, making him unable to perform his supervisory tasks.

Pursuing the happiness of others as an end is also obligatory; an important component of their happiness is secured by improvements in material welfare. In order to contribute to improvements in material welfare, *A* must avoid disabling depression.

While *A* is confronted with conflicting objective ends, it seems clear that the end of the happiness of others must be lexically prior under this set of facts. The end of developing one's capacities is objective because the agent must develop his understanding in order to be 'worthy of the humanity that dwells within him' (DV 387). It seems implausible, however, that the agent could realize his worthiness by developing his intellectual capacities while disregarding his moral obligation to realize a minimum level of social welfare for his fellow citizens. Therefore, in this context, *A* must adopt a maxim of not developing his capacities.

In order to avoid the problem of context dependence, Kant requires a principle of construction which would enable individuals to identify the morally significant characteristics of any particular set of circumstances. Such a principle of construction would enable the agent to identify, in his particular context, maxims of action which are morally or politically objective. I will argue that reflective judgment, understood as an orientational faculty, performs precisely this function.

C. The Resources of Reflective Judgment: An Ideal Criterion?

Kant describes the highest good, and therefore the kingdom of ends,[7] as an ideal of reason. An ideal is defined as an archetype which supplies a standard for reason in cases in which no determinate rule is available. The faculty of reason regards the ideal 'as being completely determinable in accordance with principles' (A571/B599).

---

[7] The kingdom of ends corresponds to the supreme good, one of the two conceptions of the highest good discussed in the *Critique of Practical Reason* (CPr 110).

Kant's account of an 'ideal', however, seems ill-suited to ground determinate propositions. In his first account of an ideal of reason (A569–71/B597–9), Kant claims that the conditions required for determination of the ideal, as required by reason, are 'not . . . to be found in experience' (A571/B599). Therefore, an ideal cannot be exemplified: the effort would be 'absurd'. If the ideal must remain indeterminate, it cannot supply a criterion relevant to political deliberation.

In fact, Kant's account of practical reason appears to require the indeterminacy of any ideal of a system of final ends. The ends of Kantian practical reason exist only in a practical context. While the individual can identify moral principles to guide his choice of a maxim of action in a given context, practical reason does not supply an account of moral ends in the absence of empirically given circumstances. Therefore, while an agent confers value on certain ends through his rational choice of those ends (see Korsgaard 1986: 186–90), no theoretical or abstract account of a system of ends seems possible. Kant appears to lack the resources to provide a determinate account of a final system of moral ends (see Yovel 1980: 141 ff.)

Moreover, Kantian practical reason seems ill-suited for the determination of collective ends: the moral law determines the *individual's* choice of maxim, and the related end, in a specific context. Yet, as Kant recognizes, maxims properly chosen from the individual perspective may fail to be appropriate when viewed from a collective standpoint (CJ 293). Kantian morality does not appear to provide a basis for determining norms to govern the collective practices of a society.

If the ideal of a unified system of moral ends is to have a practical role in political deliberation, Kant must explain how an ideal can exemplify the determinate social implications of his moral theory. In order to provide such an explanation, Kant must argue that: (i) practical reason grounds *collective* ends; and (ii) ideals are, contrary to Kant's earlier assertions (A570/B598), exemplifiable. Kant develops the resources for these arguments in the *Critique of Judgment*.

(i) The Sensus Communis *and Collective Ends*

In Kant's moral philosophy, practical principles take on determinate content only when applied by an individual in a particular context. Thus, the moral law has no substantive (as opposed to formal) content in the absence of an individual agent applying formal principles in concrete practical circumstances (actual or hypothetical).

If practical reason is to determine a system of *collective* ends, then some faculty of the mind must be capable of comparing and systematizing particular judgments made by individuals (in this case, moral ends generated in individual moral deliberation). Such a faculty would allow political judgment to avoid 'the illusion that arises from the ease of mistaking our subjective and private conditions for objective ones' (CJ 293).

In the *Critique of Judgment*, Kant argues that such a comparative faculty is a necessary condition of cognition (CJ 292). *Reflective judgment* reflects on the shareability of our cognitions or judgments before we cognize or consciously judge. Such a form of judgment presupposes a sense, the *sensus communis*, which enables us to '[take into] account (a priori) . . . everyone else's way of presenting [something], in order *as it were* to compare our own judgment with human reason in general' (CJ 293). In employing this faculty, we take account of the 'merely possible judgments of others', attending 'solely to the formal features of our presentation' (CJ 294).

Such an account might suggest that the *sensus communis* merely involves increased abstraction, the adoption of what modern ethical philosophers have labelled the 'impersonal standpoint'. In fact, Kant seems to encourage such a view in certain passages: the individual 'overrides the private subjective conditions of his judgment into which so many others are locked, as it were, and reflects on his own judgment from a *universal standpoint*' (CJ 295). Yet the individual achieves standpoint 'only by transferring himself to the standpoint of others' (CJ 295). Kant's continued stress, in this section, on the necessity of genuine intersubjectivity in reflective judgment suggests that the *sensus communis* cannot be reduced to the abstract adoption of an impersonal standpoint.

While the argument for the *sensus communis* is presented in the context of Kant's account of aesthetic judgment, Kant argues explicitly that this faculty of judgment is a necessary condition of cognition in general: '[Reflective aesthetic judgment] occurs by means of a procedure that judgment has to carry out *to give rise even to the most ordinary experience* . . . [The pleasure arising from reflective aesthetic judgment] must necessarily rest on the same conditions in everyone, because [these conditions] are the subjective conditions *for the possibility of cognition as such*' (CJ 292, emphasis mine).

If each individual is able to compare his practical judgments with the possible judgments of all other rational beings, then each individual could, in principle, apply practical reason to determine collective social ends. In addition, if our moral sense is constitutive, supplying a formal constraint on the possible judgments of rational beings, individual accounts of a system of moral ends *could* converge on an ideal account.[8] Therefore, reflective judgment provides at least the necessary formal condition for the possibility of determining social norms and, therefore, social objective ends.

Since reflective judgment takes account of the merely *formal* features of the judgments of others, reflective judgment does not, in itself, provide the basis for a complete substantive determination of a system of objective ends. Such a substantive determination must, in addition, take into account the empirical circumstances of judgment and the contingent factors influencing the judgments of individual agents. Therefore, a system of ends could only be specified by applying political judgment to the specific culture of a particular society at a particular time.

Reflective judgment does, however, appear to provide the basis for a substantive determination of the formal principles which would characterize any system of objective ends. Since morality is constitutive, one principle would regulate the judgments of all rational agents: respect for humanity as an unconditioned value. Thus, a form of social life which embodies a system of objective ends must guarantee the necessary conditions for the realization of humanity to each member.

If the notion of a system of objective ends is best understood as an ideal criterion of justice, however, this criterion appears to impose stricter requirements of justice than Kant argues for explicitly in the *Rechtslehre*. The requirements argued for in the *Rechtslehre*, however, are requirements of legitimacy, not criteria of justice. In Chapter 1, I have argued that the metaphysical

---

[8] Kant describes reflective judgment as 'not a power to produce concepts, but a power only to compare occurring cases with concepts given it from elsewhere' (FI 225). In the case of moral principles, the 'concepts . . . from elsewhere' are constitutive principles given a priori.

principles of right specified in the *Rechtslehre* narrow possible instantiations of just political institutions to a specifiable range. Political judgment makes possible the specification of the concrete implications of these metaphysical principles for institutions and norms.

(ii) Determination of an 'Ideal'

Reflective judgment provides the basis for comparing an object in experience with 'what it *is [meant] to be*' (FI 240), as determined by an a priori concept of purpose which 'contains the basis of the object's actuality' (CJ 180). Through the employment of this faculty, it becomes possible to determine (subjectively) the systematic relation of purposive principles within nature (CJ 181 ff.). In its furthest extension, reflective judgment appears to provide a basis for the evaluation of complex organized entities, including societies and forms of social life, with reference to their underlying purposive concepts (CJ 429–36).

In evaluating such a complex entity, reflective judgment first identifies the purposive concept which the object embodies. Once the underlying purposive concept has been identified, it should be possible to construct an ideal account of the entity which exemplifies the concept. Reflective judgment, therefore, appears to provide the conceptual resources necessary to transform the notion of an 'ideal' from a regulative to a practical concept (see Makkreel 1990: 117–18).

While Kant does not develop this line of argument in the *Critique of Judgment*, Kant's political and religious writings from the decade following the *Critique* explore the implications of such an argument. In a remarkable reversal of his claims in the *Critique of Pure Reason*, Kant argues that ideals are, in fact, appropriate objects for exemplification.[9] In fact, exemplification of moral ideals may be necessary in order to cultivate a moral disposition.[10] This evolution

---

[9] 'In the ascent from the sensible to the supersensible, it is indeed allowable to *schematize* (that is to render a concept intelligible by the help of an analogy to something sensible)' (R 59 n.). 'An experience [must] be possible in which [an archetype of moral perfection] is presented' (R 56).

[10] '[M]an can frame to himself no concept of the degree and strength of a force like that of a moral disposition except by picturing it' (R 55). '[I]t cannot be a matter of unconcern to morality as to whether or not it forms for itself the concept of a final end of all things . . . for only thereby can objective reality be given to the union of the purposiveness arising from freedom and the purposiveness of nature (R 5).

in the notion of an 'ideal' appears to ground Kant's teleological arguments in the late political works.

Thus, the notion of reflective judgment provides the basis for the transformation of the principle of teleology and the notion of an ideal from regulative to practical concepts. Clearly, the sketch presented here merely argues for the plausibility of a political faculty of judgment grounded in the *sensus communis*. In the following chapters, I will explore the methodology of political judgment. In the remainder of this chapter, I will consider the objections that: (i) a specified ideal constitutes a material ground of the will, and is thus inconsistent with Kant's critique of hedonic principles of legislation; and (ii) Kant's argument for rational faith explicitly limits the highest good to an unattainable object.

3. THE CRITIQUE OF HEDONIC PRINCIPLES AND KANT'S HEURISTIC CRITERION FOR POLITICAL JUDGMENT

In his moral philosophy, Kant argues unequivocally that moral motivation is defined by: (i) independence from all desired ends; and (ii) 'determination of choice by the mere form of giving a universal law' (CPr 33). Moreover, in 'Theory and Practice' and the *Rechtslehre*, Kant grounds his critique of hedonic principles of legislation in his requirement that the will must be determined by merely formal principles (see Chapter 2). These arguments might appear inconsistent with Kant's notion of objective ends and his claim that ethics is 'the system of *ends* of pure practical reason' (DV 381).

The apparent inconsistency of these claims is easily resolved in Kant's moral theory. Kantian moral motivation must be determined by the form of the maxim, not the desired end. But Kant is careful to specify that desire for the objective end does not affect the agent's motivation. Rather, the agent recognizes such an end as mandatory because it is the end associated with an obligatory maxim.

In Kant's political theory, the issue is more complicated. Ends are still obligatory only because they are associated with an obligatory maxim. Obligatory political ends, however, form a unified set which defines an ideal notion of civil association. Kant claims that moral agents have an obligation to realize an approximation of the form of social existence defined by the system of objective ends.

In this account, Kant might seem to suggest that desire for the system of ends *should* motivate action to achieve an approximation of that system. If such a reading were correct, Kant would require heteronomous motivation in his political theory, despite his claim that moral motivation must be independent of heteronomous desire.

In fact, Kant does not argue that moral agents should be motivated by desire. The system of objective ends is a system of ends each of which the agent has a duty to realize. The agent pursues each end, and thus the entire system, because each end is associated with an obligatory maxim.

While the systematic organization of ends does *not* motivate the agent, it operates as a *heuristic*, revealing social implications of Kant's moral theory which might remain unrecognized if the objective ends were considered singly, rather than as members of a unified system. Once the set of objective ends is identified, its structural characteristics can be studied.

The form of public life defined by the system of objective ends can serve as an ideal criterion by which existing norms and institutions can be judged. An individual acting upon the implications of such a judgment grounds his action in rational principle (the rational imperative[11] to realize the highest good), not in an inclination grounded in an empirical object.

Rather than motivating through inclination, the system provides a critical tool which can reveal the political implications of pure practical reason. This notion of an ideal theory which provides a criterion for non-ideal institutions thus anticipates Rawls's claim that 'ideal theory . . . provides, I believe, the only basis for the systematic grasp' of the problems of a non-ideal society (Rawls 1971: 9).

4. THE DISTINCT STATUS OF POLITICAL TELEOLOGY

Kant's application of teleological methods to the specification of political ends has been criticized as inconsistent with his account of

---

[11] 'It is a priori (morally) necessary to bring forth the highest good through freedom of the will' (CPr 113).

moral teleology in the *Critique of Practical Reason* and other writings on moral philosophy. While the role of teleology shifts radically from the moral to the political theory, Kant retains the central premisses of the moral teleology: (i) each obligatory moral maxim is necessarily connected to an obligatory end (DV 385, R 4, 6 n.); (ii) a complete set of obligatory ends would constitute a unified system grounded in the notion of autonomy (G 433, R 4, 6 n., 89); and (iii) all moral agents are committed to the realization, in some sense, of this system of ends (CJ 450; R 5, 89; see TPP 122–3, 130; MJ 354–5).

While retaining much of the basic structure of his earlier argument, however, Kant transforms the status of the principle of teleology (from regulative to reflective) and of the final ends of teleology (from a formal implication of the account of practical reason to a determinable goal which structures, but does not motivate, the moral action necessary for its realization). Thus, Kant's political theory presents teleology as a practical concept. The argument for perpetual peace and its constituent elements is to provide an additional factor to be weighed by the agent when he deliberates practically concerning political questions.

It is important to stress the conceptual shift which is necessary before the moral teleology of the *Groundwork* and the *Critique of Practical Reason* can ground a political theory. In the earlier moral teleology, the notion of a system of moral ends merely represents the claim that all objective moral ends must be commonly grounded in practical rationality. Under such an account, a system of ends would simply constitute an aggregate of the obligatory ends of moral beings. The representation of such an aggregate would have no practical significance.

In the political teleology, however, the representation of a system of moral ends constitutes a determinate goal to which the agent is committed by virtue of being a rational being. If some features of the system of moral ends are institutional, then all moral beings must be committed to the realization of such institutions. Thus, Kant's argument for political teleology is only consistent and plausible if political teleology is recognized as distinct from moral teleology.

In this section I will argue that: (i) Kant's argument for moral teleology is, in fact, most persuasive when recast as an argument for faith in moral progress towards perpetual peace, a political approximation of the highest good realizable in experience; and (ii) Kant's (practical) argument for perpetual peace is distinct and separate from Kant's (ideal) argument for rational faith in a supreme reason.

A. The Argument for Rational Faith and Political Teleology

The moral argument identifies the highest good as a logical implication of Kant's moral theory with little determinate significance for practical deliberation (see discussion in section 1). Kant's argument for rational faith (CPr 110 ff., CJ 447 ff.), however, extends the moral argument, transforming the highest good into an object of actual human striving in history.

The argument for rational faith is grounded in the claim that furthering the highest good is 'an a priori necessary' end of the moral will[12] (CPr 114, 122). The realization of this end is a 'practical necessity' for the moral will. Yet the natural order contains no causality sufficient to guarantee that moral action will in fact further the highest good.[13] In order to resolve this antinomy of practical reason, the agent is licensed to believe in a supreme reason which supplies the connection between virtue and proportionate happiness necessary to secure the highest good (CJ 450).[14]

Kant distinguishes two conceptions of the highest good: the *supreme* good and the *perfect* good (CPr 110). Only the perfect good, in which happiness proportional to virtue is realized, requires the postulate of a supreme reason to secure its realization. In the

[12] '[F]urthering of the highest good, *which contains this connection [between virtue and happiness] in its concept*, is an a priori necessary object of our will and is inseparably related to the moral law' (CPr 114, emphasis mine).

[13] '[N]o necessary connection, sufficient to the highest good, between happiness and virtue in the world can be expected from the most meticulous observation of the moral law. Since, now, the furthering of the highest good, which contains this connection in its concept, is an a priori necessary object of our will and is inseparably related to the moral law, the impossibility of the highest good must prove the falsity of the moral law also' (CPr 113–14).

[14] '[T]he concept of the *practical necessity* of [achieving] such a purpose by applying our forces does not harmonize with the theoretical concept of the *physical possibility* of its being achieved, if the causality of nature is the only causality (of a means [for achieving it]) that we connect with our freedom. Hence, in order to set ourselves a final purpose in conformity with the moral law, we must assume a moral cause of the world (an author of the world)' (CJ 450).

argument for rational faith, Kant asserts that the real possibility of realizing the *perfect* good is necessary to ground moral motivation.[15]

I will argue below that Kant fails to establish the necessity of realizing what he characterizes as the perfect, as opposed to the supreme, good. Yet, it is only the realization of the perfect good which requires the postulate of a supreme reason. Thus, I will argue, Kant's argument for rational faith demonstrates the necessity of faith in the possibility of moral progress, rather than the necessity of faith in the existence of a supreme reason.

Kant asserts that an agent cannot have confidence that his actions, alone, will further the highest (perfect) good, even if he grounds his practical decisions in moral maxims. The effect of the agent's activity in the phenomenal world depends on natural laws and the behaviour of other agents (CPr 113–14, CJ 452). Yet the realization of the perfect good requires the realization of a specific outcome: happiness in proportion to virtue. Therefore, even a 'righteous man . . . who actively reveres the moral law' must abandon the purposes of morality unless he can assume the existence of an agency who links moral actions to just outcomes (CJ 452).

While Kant's explicit argument focuses on the formal problem of a possible antinomy of practical reason, his real concern appears to be the threat to moral motivation. The basis of the agent's moral motivation may be undermined if he is unable to believe that his actions can further the highest good, because the moral agent is motivated by a conception of himself as an active agency, and thus a determining force in the phenomenal world. If the agent's actions are not effective in promoting the necessary object of the moral will, the agent's conception of himself is revealed as illusory. The necessary connection between moral action and just result is, therefore, required to preserve the agent's conception of himself as an intelligible causality. Without such a conception, the agent will not take an interest in being motivated by the moral law (see Korsgaard 1989). Yet this argument will ground the postulate of a

---

[15] 'That virtue (as the worthiness to be happy) is the supreme condition of whatever appears to us to be desirable . . . and, consequently that it is the supreme good have been proved in the Analytic. But these truths do not imply that virtue is the entire and perfect good as the object of the faculty of desire of rational finite beings. For this, happiness is also required . . . the highest good always means the whole, the perfect good' (CPr 110).

supreme reason only if the necessary object of the moral will must be the perfect, rather than the supreme good.

Kant does not justify his assertion that furthering the perfect good, rather than supreme good, is the necessary condition of moral motivation. The supreme good consists of a state of affairs in which all agents act from moral motivation, but such moral motivation does not guarantee proportional happiness. In the *Groundwork*, Kant describes this state as the kingdom of ends. Unlike the perfect good, the kingdom of ends is realizable through the moral action of individuals, regardless of the effects of natural forces and the acts of other agents. Thus, the kingdom of ends can be viewed as the 'secular counterpart' of the perfect good (see Rawls n.d.: Lecture 9, p. 3).

In fact, it is arguable that the possibility of furthering the realization of a kingdom of ends should provide a sufficient condition for moral motivation. Kant asserts that the good will is good 'without qualification' (G 393). In addition, the value of the good will is universally recognized in ordinary views of morality. If all agents recognize the absolute value of a good will, then acting to further the kingdom of ends, in which all agents act from good will, is acting to further the highest good any agent can know in the sensible world.

While a finitely rational being must regard a state of affairs in which virtuous rational beings achieve happiness proportionate to their moral merit as superior to a similar state of affairs in which the virtuous do not achieve proportionate happiness (CPr 110–11), this claim does not establish that the *realization* of happiness proportionate to virtue must be the necessary end of the moral will. Even if natural forces or agencies intervene to prevent actions grounded in good will from achieving happiness proportionate to virtue, the furtherance of the kingdom of ends (as good 'without qualification') must be sufficient in itself to motivate moral action, without regard for the practical consequences. Each individual agent could be confident that his choice to ground his actions in moral motives would, by definition, further the achievement of a kingdom of ends.[16] Therefore, if the realization of a kingdom of ends is an absolute value, the possibility of realizing such a state of affairs

---

[16] Since the kingdom of ends is a state of the world in which all agents act from good will, the decision of each agent to act from good will furthers the realization of the kingdom of ends by increasing the number of agents motivated by good will.

should provide a sufficient ground for moral interest. If the possibility of furthering the kingdom of ends, rather than the perfect good, is necessary for moral motivation, then the rational faith argument can be recast. Faith in such a possibility does not require the postulate of a supreme reason. Since all rational beings experience moral motivation, the realization of the kingdom of ends *could* be achieved entirely through human agency. Realizing this end simply requires that all moral agents act from the moral motivation they experience. Since all rational beings are *capable* of acting from moral motivation,[17] such a state of affairs is manifestly possible within the natural order.

Since humans are not perfectly rational, human beings will predictably fail to act entirely from moral motivation. Therefore, rational faith is still required in order to sustain moral motivation. But the object of the faith has changed. Rather than faith in a supreme reason, the necessary postulate is now one of moral progress and the perfectibility of man's moral nature. Kant appears to reconceive the moral faith argument in this fashion when he argues that doubting our joint capacity to work towards perpetual peace (*rather than* the highest good) 'would give rise to the execrable wish to dispense with all reason and to regard ourselves, along with our principles, as subject to the same mechanism of nature as the other animal species' (MJ 355). Therefore, in order to sustain moral motivation, it is necessary that we maintain faith in joint capacity to sustain 'infinite progress towards complete fitness' to the moral law (CPr 122).[18]

Moreover, Kant's moral theory provides some basis for such rational faith. Each individual experiences moral motivation by virtue of the fact that he is a rational being with a will. As such an entity, he is subject to moral imperatives. Since all other humans are also rational agents possessing a will, the agent has reason to

---

[17] '[W]hen the moral law commands that we *ought* now to be better men, it follows inevitably that we must *be able* to be better men' (R 46). '[I]t is patently absurd to say that we *cannot* act as the moral law requires. For if this were so, the concept of duty would automatically be dropped from morals' (TPP 116).

[18] Moreover, in the *Critique of Judgment*, Kant claims that: '[t]he moral law . . . determines for us, and a priori, a final purpose, and makes it obligatory for us to strive toward it; and that purpose is the *highest good* in the world that we can achieve through freedom' (CJ 450). Thus Kant asserts that the final purpose is a state which we *can* achieve in this world through freedom.

believe that all other humans experience moral imperatives. Therefore, while humans as a class may be 'radically evil',[19] they are not
necessarily intentionally malevolent.[20] Each agent recognizes moral
obligation and is capable of acting from it.

In addition, Kant believes that imperfectly rational beings can
cultivate a moral disposition by acting from a second order desire
to act from moral motivation: '[M]an's moral growth of necessity
begins not in the improvement of his practices but rather in the
transforming of his cast of mind and in the grounding of a character'[21] (R 43). Not only do all humans experience moral imperatives,
but all are capable of cultivating a moral disposition. Faith in moral
progress is, therefore, firmly grounded in Kant's account of moral
nature.

Kant's political teleology is grounded in this notion of rational
faith in moral progress. The object of rational political faith, however, is 'the highest political good' (MJ 355), or perpetual peace.
Thus, unlike the *moral* rational faith argument, the *political* rational faith argument specifies a determinate account of the objective end to be realized.

While it is not clear that the political argument 'supersedes' the
moral/religious argument, the shift in the status of teleology, as a
principle, between the religious and political works suggests that
Kant's political theory addresses perceived imperfections of the
religious teleology. The moral argument for rational faith merely
allows us to conclude that the natural order 'is open to the possibility that a realm of ends should be achieved within it' (Rawls n.d.:
Lecture 9, p. 5). The moral argument provides no account of the
significance of that conclusion for practical deliberation. Thus, the
moral faith argument presents the highest good as 'immanent as
the object of volition', but still transcendent 'as an idea of reason'
(Silber 1959: 487). In the *political* teleology, as I argue in section 2,

---

[19] Kant does not define 'radical evil' as 'repudiat[ing] the moral law in the manner
of a rebel' (R 31). Rather, radical evil consists in 'mak[ing] the incentive of self-love
and its inclinations the condition of obedience to the moral law' (R 32). This evil is
'radical . . . because it corrupts the ground of all maxims' (R 32).
[20] 'Man (even the most wicked) does not, under any maxim whatever, repudiate
the moral law in the manner of a rebel . . . The law, rather, forces itself upon him
irresistibly by virtue of his moral disposition; and were no other incentive working
in opposition, he would adopt the law into his supreme maxim' (R 31).
[21] 'Virtue in this sense is won *little by little* and . . . requires long practice' (R 42).

the 'highest political good' is immanent *both* as an object of volition *and* as an ideal of reason.

B. Status of Political Teleology

In Kant's accounts of the philosophy of history and religion, the highest good is defined as the idea of a state of affairs in which perfect virtue is united with perfect happiness. The practical approximation of the highest good proposed by the political teleology would be characterized by neither perfect happiness nor perfect virtue.

If perpetual peace (and its constituent elements, such as republican government) does not involve the unification of perfect virtue with perfect happiness, in what sense can it be said to be an approximation of the highest good? Perpetual peace does not instantiate the unification of these two values, but it does embody the synthesis of both values.

The political institutions constitutive of perpetual peace structure incentives for action so that all members act as though motivated by purely moral incentives. Such a structured set of incentives 'genuinely makes it much easier for the moral capacities of men to develop into an immediate respect for right' (TPP 121 n.).

Political institutions therefore perform a mediating role, eliciting moral motivation from participants: 'we cannot ripen to . . . freedom if we are not first of all placed therein (we must be free in order to make purposive use of our powers of freedom)' (R 176–7 n.). As Riley (1983) argues, in Kant's account of politics, legality and culture is 'midway . . . between nature and freedom . . . prepar[ing] the way . . . for self determination through "ought" and "objective ends" ' (80).

While perpetual peace may not be characterized by the instantiation of perfect virtue, it does embody the institutions which make possible moral evolution that approximates perfect virtue as closely as is possible for imperfectly rational agents. In providing the context for moral evolution, these institutions also provide the context for realization of the highest-order happiness associated with realizing one's rational nature (CPr 116, R 19 n.). In fully realizing his rational nature, the individual experiences the greatest measure of this highest-order happiness. Therefore, while perpetual peace does not instantiate the unification of perfect virtue with perfect happiness, it does instantiate the progressive synthesis of moral motivation and the highest-order happiness associated with the realization of rational freedom.

Moreover, the political teleology of perpetual peace vindicates the possibility of political practical deliberation, as the moral teleology of rational faith vindicates the possibility of acting from moral motivation (individual practical deliberation). The rational faith argument is significant in Kant's philosophy because it satisfies what Kant took to be an essential need of practical reason: the need to provide an account of the practical efficacy of moral motivation. The rational faith argument is intended to demonstrate that such efficacy is possible. Since we have grounds for practical belief that acting from moral motivation will ultimately secure the ends of practical reason, acting from moral motivation is not, of necessity, inefficacious.

Perpetual peace, the pragmatic approximation of the highest good, performs a different kind of motivational role. Rather than vindicating the possible efficacy of practical reason, it provides a representation of the ends of practical reason.[22] Without such a representation, moral agents would be unable to identify the requirements of practical reason in the political and legal spheres of action. Thus, while the rational faith argument vindicates the possibility of acting from moral motivation per se, perpetual peace vindicates the possibility of acting from moral motivation in the public sphere.

CONCLUSION

A traditional interpretation presents Kant's political theory as merely a formal elaboration of the concept of mutual external

---

[22] Kant seems to have experienced some uncertainty regarding the status of objective ends in politics, as opposed to ethics. Thus, in the *Doctrine of Virtue*, Kant claims that 'the concept of an *end* that is also a duty . . . belongs exclusively to ethics' (DV 389). Nevertheless, Kant invariably characterizes the political goal of perpetual peace as an objective end. In the *Rechtslehre*, Kant describes the highest political good (perpetual peace) as 'an end such that the maxim of adopting it is a duty' (MJ 354). In 'Towards Perpetual Peace', Kant characterizes perpetual peace as 'the end which man's own reason prescribes to him as a duty' (TPP 112, see 109) Finally, in the 'Theory and Practice' essay, Kant characterizes the highest political good as 'an ultimate end posited by pure reason and comprehending the totality of all ends within a single principle'; the motive to adopt this end is 'obedience to it as a duty' (TP 65).

freedom. I have argued (in Chapters 1 and 2) that this traditional interpretation is unsatisfactory. Rather, I argue, mutual external freedom constitutes merely the *necessary* condition for a rightful civil condition. The *sufficient* condition for realizing such a social goal requires that positive law embody the metaphysical principles of natural law.

Political teleology makes possible a determination of the implications of the principles of natural law for experience. Thus, the teleological approach supplements the traditional interpretation, making possible an account of the nature of a positive law which embodies the principles of natural law. In the following chapters, I will develop an account of Kant's employment of the resources of political teleology in developing an account of political reflective judgment.

4

Systematicity and Political Salience

IN Kant's account of right, I have argued, the principles of natural law must influence and constrain the content of positive law. Yet the principles of natural law are pure rational concepts (MJ 205) which by definition are not constitutive for experience.[1] In addressing this discontinuity between natural and positive laws, I have suggested, Kant's investigation of the relation between abstract rational principles and practical judgments grounds a shift in his analytic perspective, from the investigation of metaphysical principles in the *Rechtslehre* to the specification, through reflective judgment, of moral and political purposes in 'Towards Perpetual Peace'.

The status and role of reflective judgment in Kant's political thought have been the subject of considerable controversy in the contemporary Kant literature. While Arendt (1982), Beiner (1983), and Bielefeldt (1997) argue that Kant's canonical works of political theory neglect the importance of the faculty of judgment for his account of politics, Riley (1983), Makkreel (1990), and Henrich (1992) argue persuasively that reflective judgment was central to Kant's explicit political thought. While one hesitates to disagree with such eminent theorists as Arendt and Beiner, Riley (1992) argues persuasively that 'Arendt has seized upon the right work (*Judgment*) only to give it a reading it will barely bear' (311). While Arendt 'discards the actual political writings, and tries to express a politics from aesthetic judgment' (307), Kant 'really did write a political philosophy, and one which rests on *more* than the mere "general communication" of enlightened or enlarged "opinion"' (308).

I will argue that Kant's account of reflective judgment, in grounding an account of final moral and political purposes, makes

[1] '[T]he pure concepts of reason . . . are *transcendental ideas* . . . I understand by idea a necessary concept of reason to which no corresponding object can be given in sense experience' (A327/B383–4).

possible judgments specifying the practical implications of the pure rational principles of morality and right. Thus, through the faculty of reflective judgment, the nature of the influence that the pure principles of natural law exert over the content of positive law may be specified. In order to make possible practical judgments regarding the relation of natural and positive law, however, reflective judgment must specify both the moral salience of particular relations in experience (thus confronting and resolving the problem of context dependence) and the practical implications of the pure principles relevant to such relations. If reflective judgments reliably specify both moral salience and the practical implications of pure principles, then the faculty of reflective judgment will make possible practical judgments defining the relation of natural and practical law, and specifying the policy implications of the principles of natural law.

In this chapter I will claim that Kant's argument for systematicity in empirical knowledge, in the *Critique of Judgment*, grounds an account of the moral salience of relations in experience. In section 1, I will examine the functions that an account of moral salience is required to perform in political judgment. In sections 2 and 3, I will evaluate (i) the status of Kant's employment of the notion of systematicity in characterizing relations in experience; and (ii) the degree to which such a characterization can ground the specification of the moral quality of actions and purposes in experience. I will defer until Chapter 5 discussion of: (i) the methodology of practical teleological judgment; and (ii) the role of teleological judgment in specifying the significance of morally salient features of experience.

1. MORAL SALIENCE AS A PROBLEM IN KANTIAN POLITICAL JUDGMENT

An important strand in Kant's political thought requires that politics must be guided by moral ends (TPP 125, see 121–4, MJ 355). Yet political phenomena are constituted by the interactions of empirical beings in experience (see CJ 406, FI 239 ff.), while Kantian morality is a theory of pure rational concepts which, by definition, 'overstep the limits of all experience' (A327/B384). Unless moral ends can be translated into terms constitutive for the empirical world, moral theory cannot ground an account of political judgment.

If, as Kant asserts (TPP 125, 130, CF 187–9, MJ 354, CJ 196), the ends of morality are to be realized in experience, he must explain how pure principles of reason can have determinate implications for norms and institutions governing relations in experience (see CJ 196). Such an explanation is an essential precondition for the possibility of a Kantian political theory.

Kant's revision and extension of his account of objective moral ends is apparently intended to suggest a plausible link between practical reason and political judgment: the systematic relation of moral ends constitutes the basis for an ideal criterion by which political institutions can be evaluated. Yet the construction of such an ideal criterion cannot, in itself, ground a link between practical reason and political judgment. Rather, the gulf between experience and pure practical reason[2] would have to be bridged *before* a system of objective ends could be specified as an ideal criterion.

Objective ends are identified through the contradiction in the will test: if the negation of a permissible maxim cannot be universalized, the maxim and the end associated with the maxim are both obligatory. Such a hypothetical universalization necessarily relies on the agent's own characterization of a proposed action and its relation to other objects in experience. Yet in order to characterize actions and their relation to other objects with sufficient specificity to allow the universalization, the agent must be able to determine, prior to the universalization, the significance of the events being described.

Unless the agent can characterize the significance of acts and relations in experience prior to testing his maxim, the universalization tests will be indeterminate or will yield perverse results, even in relatively trivial cases. For example, suppose I play tennis at 6.00 a.m. on Sundays in order to avoid waiting for a court. Is the underlying maxim: 'to play when no one else is playing'? If so, I cannot universalize the maxim. I appear to have an obligation to make it my maxim to play when someone else is playing. But that can't be right.

Perhaps a better account of my maxim would be: 'to avoid

---

[2] '[A]n immense gulf is fixed between the domain of the concept of nature, the sensible, and the domain of the concept of freedom, the supersensible, so that no transition from the supersensible (and hence by means of the theoretical use of reason) is possible' (CJ 175–6). Experience falls within the realm of nature, while practical reason is a faculty grounded in the supersensible domain of freedom.

needless competition for court time'. But how do I know that this is the appropriate characterization of my proposed principle of action unless I have access to pre-existing norms governing the framing of maxims? It seems that moral agents must be able to identify the morally salient features of experience *before* they apply the contradiction tests which identify objective ends.

It appears, therefore, that objective ends can be specified only if practical reason can apply criteria of moral salience to circumstances *prior* to moral or political judgment. Herman (1993) argues for the necessity of such criteria in moral judgment. The need for criteria of moral salience is, if anything, more urgent for political judgment.

In order to specify the moral salience of a set of circumstances in experience, the agent must both: (i) recognize that the circumstances are relevant to a certain kind of judgment; and (ii) determine the significance of the set of circumstances for such a judgment. Thus, a specification of moral salience appears to require two operations, the first *characterizing* the circumstances in question, and the second *interpreting* that characterization. In the tennis example, I must: (i) specify the relevant characterization of my actions relative to a given state of affairs; and (ii) test the moral quality of those actions under such a characterization.

If the agent is to be able to specify the moral quality of any particular action in any set of circumstances, he must possess a faculty of judgment which permits him to order and relate possible maxims and purposes in any state of affairs. Moreover, the ordering generated must be complete and systematic over all maxims and purposes in experience. If this were not the case, the ranking would fail to preserve transitivity, leaving open the possibility that no coherent ordering could be achieved. Thus, in order to specify the moral salience of purposive maxims, the agent requires a faculty of judgment which subsumes purposive activity in experience systematically under universal principles.

In the *Critique of Judgment*, Kant argues that human reason necessarily judges the aggregate of purposive agencies in nature as a 'system of purposes' (CJ 427). This argument for systematicity as a necessary feature of human judgment appears to offer a theoretical grounding for the necessary subsumption of purposive agencies and activities in experience under universal principles. But Kant's account of systematicity has traditionally been understood as investigating theoretical, rather than practical, claims about the purposiveness manifested by complex systems existing in nature. Thus, for example, Pluhar (1987) argues that Kant's teleology, 'taken beyond the cognition of nature', merely 'confirms the moral argument . . . from a theoretical point of view' (p. lxxxv).

Two important contemporary examinations of Kantian teleology are more sensitive to the practical aspect of systematicity in Kant's teleology. Makkreel (1990) argues that teleological judgment grounds 'a kind of reflective leverage on the world . . . a mode of orientation to tradition that allows us to ascertain its relevance to ultimate questions of truth' (158–9). This form of orientation towards tradition 'allows us to relate our own standpoint to a larger perspective . . . of communal meaning' (159). Since reflective judgment illuminates the significance of our historical tradition, 'we may say that reflective interpretation is constitutive for the human sciences' (170). Guyer (1991) argues that Kant's teleological analysis grounds an argument 'unify[ing] his theoretical and practical philosophy by showing that the former can only be completed with the latter' (165).

While these recent accounts advance our understanding of Kantian teleology, I will argue in section 2 that neither Guyer nor Makkreel identifies the full practical significance of Kant's argument. In particular, neither distinguishes carefully between the two functions of teleological judgment: (i) characterization of the moral character of an object or relation in experience; and (ii) interpretation of that characterization.

I will argue that Kantian teleology plausibly grounds the kind of systematic account of purposive agencies and activities in experience necessary to ground an account of moral salience. Yet Kant presents nothing resembling a clear account of the operations of teleological judgment in specifying the moral salience of relations in experience. Kant's reticence thus places a double burden on his interpreter, who must both identify the outlines of a defensibly Kantian account and defend this account on Kantian principles.

2. SYSTEMATICITY AND EXPERIENCE

Since relations in experience are contingent, and therefore not necessarily amenable to organization under a priori universal principles, a faculty of judgment subsuming such relations under universal principles might appear to be unattainable within Kantian theory. In fact, Kant argues that it must be possible to understand nature, including empirical and contingent relations within nature, as a unified system. Reason requires that 'even the laws of nature [must] be combined in a unified and hence lawful way' (CJ 404). Moreover, 'if we think of nature as a system (as indeed we must), then experience [too] must be possible [for us] as a system even in terms of empirical laws' (FI 209). While Kant concedes that the principles of 'lawfulness of the contingent' governing our perceptions of objects in experience could not be constitutive, he nevertheless argues that such principles would hold 'just as necessarily for *human judgment*' as if they were objective principles (CJ 404).

The need for a systematic and law-governed account of relations in experience, in fact, emerges as a central concern in Kant's critical writings as early as 1781. The question of the systematicity of empirical knowledge is suggested directly by Kant's account of the faculty of reason and its employment. Reason is defined as 'the faculty which secures the unity of the rules of the understanding under principles' (A302/B359).[3] Reason achieves this unity by freeing concepts of the understanding 'from the unavoidable limitations of possible experience . . . by carrying the empirical synthesis as far as the unconditioned' (A409/B435–6). That is, reason requires the unconditioned completion of any sequence of conditioned judgments (A307–9/B364–5, Bxx).[4]

In requiring the unity of the knowledge of the understanding, freed from the limitations of experience, reason thus requires that 'the knowledge obtained by the understanding . . . is to be not a mere contingent aggregate, but a system connected according to necessary laws' (A645/B673). Reason, therefore, requires an unconditioned account of the systematic interrelation of all knowledge of the understanding. Since knowledge is only achieved when particular impressions are subsumed under concepts of the understanding, reason requires a systematic account of all impressions

---

[3] The understanding determines sensible impressions under concepts, or rules, and thus 'work[s] up the raw material of the sensible impressions into that knowledge of objects which is entitled experience' (B1). Reason functions solely to unify the concepts of the understanding, and therefore never applies directly to experience.

[4] See A409/B438, A498/B526, A509/B537, A516/B544, A646/B674, A832/B860.

(representations of the objects of possible experience) which are subsumable under concepts.

Moreover, since experience is rendered *intelligible* only by the faculty of reason,[5] we 'must view nature as constructed in accordance with [reason's] own needs so far as this is necessary to render nature accessible to reason's exploration' (Neiman 1994: 64–5) In this sense, systematicity is a necessary presupposition of all scientific investigations of the objects and relations in experience. Such a presupposition does not constitute a hypothesis which can be confirmed by facts, but rather a demand of reason which scientific inquiry must satisfy[6] (see A645–6/B673–4; Neiman 1994: 64–7).

Kant employs the notion of systematicity in two senses. The first sense involves interconnections among basic substances and empirical laws: the laws of nature must form a logical system. Kant had argued in the *Critique of Pure Reason* that this sense of systematicity was a necessary condition of experience (A216/B263). The second sense refers to a systematic unity which could exist among objects and their relations in experience. The existence of a logical and systematic relation between the laws of nature does not guarantee that the objects which these laws govern, and their relations in experience, will actually instantiate a systematic form of purposiveness (see McFarland 1970: 14–15, 92–6). Yet systematicity is a necessary presupposition of scientific inquiry in general, and is not limited to inquiries regarding fundamental laws of nature. Thus, Kant claims that the second sense of systematicity is a 'condition for the possibility of the understanding itself' (Guyer 1990: 29, see A653–4/B681–2).

In the first edition of the *Critique of Pure Reason*, Kant argues that systematicity, in the second sense, is secured by 'an objective ground which makes it impossible that appearances should be apprehended by the imagination other than under the condition of a possible synthetic unity of this apprehension' (A121). This

---

[5] While the understanding 'work[s] up' impressions into knowledge, the understanding merely 'represents things as they are, without considering whether and how we can obtain knowledge of them' (A498/B526–7).

[6] 'This unity of reason always presupposes an idea, namely that of a form of a whole of knowledge . . . This idea accordingly postulates a complete unity in the knowledge obtained by the understanding . . . These concepts of reason are not derived from nature; on the contrary, we interrogate nature in accordance with these ideas, and consider our knowledge as defective so long as it is not adequate to them' (A645–6/B673–4).

'ground', which Kant calls 'affinity', is 'objectively necessary', since it is necessary for the unity of apperception, and thus for 'all possible perception' (A122). The necessity of such a ground does not give rise to a transcendental principle, however, since affinity is not a condition which objects must satisfy in order to be subjects of possible cognition, but rather a condition which empirical consciousness must supply in order to make apprehension of objects possible.[7] Thus, in the first edition, systematicity is a quality supplied by consciousness, not necessarily a quality of objects (see A665/B693). Systematicity therefore constitutes a regulative ideal, rather than a transcendental principle.

Kant, however, was ultimately unsatisfied with the first edition's account of systematicity. The discussion of affinity is dropped from the second edition (1885), and an entirely new account of systematicity is offered in the *Critique of Judgment* (1890).[8]

In the First Introduction to the third *Critique*, Kant argues for a transcendental principle of the systematicity of nature.[9] Natural forms and laws might be so diverse that we *could not* identify the

---

[7] Guyer (1990) notes that at least one passage in the *Critique of Pure Reason* goes beyond such a claim: 'without [unity according to principles in nature], we could not even have reason, without this however no coherent use of the understanding, and in the absence of this no adequate criterion of empirical truth.' Therefore, we must 'presuppose the systematic unity of nature as objectively valid and necessary throughout' (A651/B679). As Guyer points out, however, Kant 'does not explain how or why systematicity is required in order to have an empirical criterion of truth'. In fact, 'most of what he says in the first *Critique* suggests that the understanding *can* succeed in subsuming empirical intuitions under empirical concepts without reference to any constraint of systematicity' (Guyer 1990: 28).

[8] Several passages in the first *Critique* suggest the basis for Kant's dissatisfaction. For example, Kant argues that it is difficult 'to understand how there can be a logical principle by which reason prescribes the unity of rules, unless we also presuppose a transcendental principle whereby such a systematic unity is *a priori* assumed to be necessarily inherent in objects' (A650/B678, see A651/B679, A653–4/B681–2). While Kant does not develop the logical implications of this concern in the first *Critique*, they occupy his attention throughout the third *Critique*.

[9] '[T]he empirical laws might be so diverse and heterogeneous that, though we might on occasion discover particular laws in terms of which we could connect some perceptions to [form] an experience, we could never bring these empirical laws themselves under a common principle . . . We would be unable to do this if—as is surely possible intrinsically . . . these laws, as well as the natural forms conforming to them, were infinitely diverse and heterogeneous and manifested themselves to us in a crude chaotic aggregate without the slightest trace of a system . . . if we think of nature as a system (as indeed we must), then . . . it is subjectively necessary [for us to make the] transcendental *presupposition* that nature does not have this disturbing boundless heterogeneity . . . Now this presupposition is the transcendental principle of judgment' (FI 209).

principles (e.g. empirical concepts) governing the diverse empirical laws. Yet in order to secure the possibility of experience, we must be able to identify empirical concepts and apply them to empirical intuitions. If we are unable to identify concepts unless objects actually satisfy the requirement of systematic unity, then systematicity requires a transcendental principle.[10]

As Guyer (1990) argues persuasively, presupposing the existence of lawlike relations among empirical objects is not sufficient to guarantee that natural laws will be subsumable under higher-order principles: 'a universe of recurring but non-systematic shapes, colors, or tones . . . would suffice for the application of a set of empirical general concepts without yielding any *system* of classifications' (29). Thus, it is the task of the faculty of judgment 'to attempt to apply the pure concepts of the understanding to empirical intuitions through intermediate empirical concepts which represent a systematization of our experience, and it must at least presuppose that what we are given is sufficiently systematizable for it to pursue such an objective rationally' (35).

The faculty of judgment must therefore generate the 'intermediate empirical concepts' necessary to systematize empirical experience, thus making cognition possible.[11] In order to generate such intermediate concepts, judgment must subsume objects in the external world under principles. Thus, it is judgment's task to generate concepts to subsume objects for which the understanding lacks concepts. Yet knowledge of objects is only possible *after* the understanding has determined the object under a concept. How is judgment to systematize objects to which it has no direct cognitive access?

Judgment's project is possible within the critical system because

---

[10] Reflective judgment, as a subjective principle, and its maxims 'is necessary in order that we may cognize natural laws in experience. For these maxims allow us to arrive at concepts, even if these were to be concepts of reason; and reflective judgment needs such concepts whenever it seeks so much as to get to know nature in terms of its empirical laws' (CJ 386).

[11] The organization of impressions of objects under concepts is, in fact, an essential function of both the understanding and judgment. The understanding must identify the concepts under which it determines sensible impressions. The understanding identifies these concepts by comparing schemata of objects and 'sift[ing] the sensible given with an eye to generating concepts to be bound in judgments' (Longuenesse 1998: 111). While concepts are generated through comparison, a concept nevertheless 'represents something "present in itself" in the object' (Longuenesse 1998: 120).

of the nature of the principles which judgment is to generate. Such principles are not to constitute valid truth claims about experience. Rather, such principles are to satisfy the requirement of reason for a kind of explanatory transparency which satisfies the demand for systematic relation and lawlike order: 'We settle for regarding natural purposes as objects that are explicable solely in terms of natural laws that must be conceived of by using the idea of purposes as principle' (CJ 383). Thus, we bring teleological judgment into our investigation 'so as to bring nature under principles of observation and investigation by *analogy* with the causality in terms of purposes' (CJ 360).

While reason demands a regress to the unconditioned ('the complete series of conditions') for every given conditioned determination (A498/B526), the end-point of such a regress is 'a point which is absolutely necessary' (Neiman 1995: 22), not a true proposition. Since the required form of necessity is necessity-for-human-reason, the end-point must provide an end to the regress which renders the world 'perfectly transparent to reason' (22). Thus, the required intermediate empirical concepts may render the world transparent, and hold necessarily for human judgment (CJ 404), without claiming to provide theoretical knowledge of objects in experience.

The pursuit of this end-point might, however, seem to indulge in a fallacy of traditional metaphysics which Kant criticizes. While the regress to the unconditioned is 'set as a task', we cannot 'infer the absolute totality of the series' from a mere appearance. The traditional error, which Kant wishes to correct, was to take the conditioned as a thing in itself, rather than an appearance (A499/B527). Such an error involves taking the matter of the conditioned as given. To take the *form* of the conditioned as given, however, is to reason consistently with Kant's critical theory (see Longuenesse 1995: 115–20).

The faculty of reflective judgment specifies the purposive principle implicit in an object's form. Either the object's purposiveness is manifest in 'the harmony of the form of the object . . . with the cognitive powers', or it is manifest 'as the harmony of the form of the object with the possibility of the thing itself according to a prior concept of the thing that contains the basis for that form' (CJ 192).

A particular empirical object, intrinsically, 'contains something contingent' (CJ 404). Therefore, the form of such objects must reflect contingent, rather than universal principles[12] (CJ 407). Kant defines lawful relations among contingent objects or principles as 'purposiveness'.[13] This is because human reason necessarily regards a 'real whole of nature' as the joint effect of its component parts. Thus, we must view the possibility of the parts as determined by a 'presentation' of the whole which contains 'the basis that makes possible the form of the whole as well as the connection of the parts'. Since Kant defines a purpose as 'the product of a cause that determines its effect merely on the basis of the presentation of that effect', the relation of contingent parts to the whole is 'purposive' (CJ 407–8). Thus, in order to interpret the formal qualities of empirical objects, and to determine a systematic subsumptive logic governing such objects in experience, judgment must employ 'the concept of purposiveness' as an organizing principle 'under which it can subsume that particular' (CJ 404).

Kant discusses two forms of reflective judgment. In aesthetic judgment, we lack a universal concept adequate to ground an aesthetic judgment and must evaluate an object in experience by 'ascend[ing] from the particular in nature to the universal' (CJ 180). In teleological judgment, we specify the purposive principle implicit in the form of an empirical object, but we have no intuition of a form of causality adequate to instantiate the principle in experience (CJ 192).

Of these two forms of reflective judgment, only teleological judgment provides a determinate evaluation of the purposive orientation of a complex object in experience. In teleological judgment we compare two concepts of an empirical object: (i) the object as it 'is'; and (ii) the object as it *'is [meant] to be'* (FI 240). In comparing these two concepts of the object, we 'judge the real (objective) purposiveness of nature' implicit in the form of the object (CJ 193).

Teleological judgment is theoretically problematic because an empirical concept must be assigned to the object *before* judgment

---

[12] 'Our understanding . . . [requires] contingency [in the combination of the parts in order to make a determinable form of the whole possible], because it must start from the parts taken as bases—which are thought of as universal—for different possible forms that are to be subsumed under these bases as consequences. [We], given the character of our understanding, can regard a real whole of nature only as the joint effect of the motive forces of the parts' (CJ 407).

[13] 'The lawfulness of the contingent is called purposiveness' (CJ 404).

has occurred.[14] This empirical concept is necessary because it provides the basis for evaluating the object's form as the instantiation of a kind of purposive principle. To identify this initial empirical concept, we must assign a certain kind of relevance to an object as an *input* to judgment. That is, we must assign this relevance to the object *before* we judge it, as a precondition of employing the faculty of judgment: 'we presuppose a concept of the object, and judge [how] the object is possible in terms of a law about the connection of causes and effects' (FI 234).

The problem of specifying the initial, prejudgmental concept is formally equivalent to the problem of specifying moral salience. In each case, we must assign a kind of relevance to empirical objects *before* we have judged them.

But what warrant do we have to assign such a concept to an object of experience? Neither of the two faculties of judgment (the imagination and the understanding) is equipped to specify the necessary concept. The imagination is not a faculty of concepts; and the understanding is a faculty of pure concepts which have no direct relation to particular objects in experience.[15]

The concepts of the object employed in teleological judgment must therefore be concepts of reason. Thus, as Kant concedes, teleological judgment must go beyond the faculties constitutive of judgment and 'put the understanding in a relation to reason' (FI 233).

In cases in which a sensible input can be determined under the a priori concepts of the understanding, the imagination forms a 'singular representation' of sensible impressions which 'relates immediately' to the object[16] (A320/B377); and the understanding

---

[14] 'Here, our judging of the object's possibility is based on a concept (of a purpose) that precedes a priori [that purpose]' (FI 240).

[15] '[O]ur understanding determines nothing regarding the diversity of the particular' (CJ 407).

[16] This description appears to be in tension with Kant 's account of a 'representation' as involving determination under a concept (A51/B75): since the imagination does not determine intuitions under concepts, it should be incapable of providing a 'representation'. Allison (1983) argues that this tension can be resolved by specifying the precise nature of the representation constituted by the imagination: 'although intuitions do not in fact represent or refer to objects apart from being "brought under concepts" in a judgment, they *can* be brought under concepts, and when they are they *do* represent particular objects. In this respect, they differ from purely subjective or aesthetic "representations" . . . it is really necessary to draw a distinction between determinate or conceptualized and indeterminate or unconceptualized intuitions' (Allison 1983: 67–8).

determines this representation under an a priori concept. If a sensible impression cannot be determined under an a priori concept of the understanding, however, judgment provides 'the *rule* for using the concept of purposes' in the direct determination of objects after the 'transcendental principle [of the formal purposiveness of nature] has already prepared the understanding to apply the concept of a purpose (at least in terms of form) to nature' (CJ 193–4).

Reason's concept of purposiveness is, therefore, necessary for the determination of phenomena of experience when no pure concept of the understanding is applicable: reason's concept of purposiveness 'is necessary for human judgment in dealing with nature', and by implication, with empirical phenomena in general (CJ 404).

Specification of the two concepts of the object necessary for teleological judgment requires distinct employments of reason's concept of purposiveness. The concept of what the object 'is' requires a specification of the purposive principle underlying the object, that is a specification of the object's purposive form. The concept of what the object 'is meant to be' requires specification of the significance of this form. Here, judgment must relate the formal purposiveness of the object to a specification of the systematic relation of purposes in nature and exhibit the significance of that relation. In exhibiting the significance of this relation,[17] the judgment specifies the moral salience of the object, thus satisfying the necessary condition for Kantian political judgment.

3. CHARACTERIZING THE FORM OF OBJECTS AND RELATIONS IN EXPERIENCE

In his discussion of the concept of a purpose of nature, Kant identifies the circumstances in which the assignment of a purposive concept to an object is warranted for teleological judgment. Kant's argument here is of central importance to his account of teleological judgment because he specifies the single set of conditions under which we are warranted in assigning a purposive concept to the form of a phenomenon in experience. We are au-thorized to make such an assignment because of the interaction of constraints on

---

[17] Between (i) the purposive principle implicit in the form of the object and (ii) purposes on nature.

human understanding which narrow the set of possible determinations to such an extent that we are forced to make a specific,
if merely subjective, judgment.

Kant's discussion of purposes of nature is presented in the
context of an account of the scientific applications of teleological
judgment. This fact might suggest that Kant intended his discussion
of this notion and its implications for teleological judgment
in general to be limited to theoretical applications. In fact, Kant
presents teleological judgment as a faculty which plays an important and necessary role in (i) the interpretation of the significance
of historical events, and (ii) the determination of political goals.
Sections 61–78 of the *Critique of Judgment* provide Kant's only
account of the basic structural features of this faculty, and Kant
appears to rely on this account in applying teleological judgment to
historical and political matters in the Appendix to the *Critique of
Judgment*, and in his later essays.

Since Kant provides an explicit account of the structure and
function of teleological judgment in sections 61–78, and proceeds
to apply this faculty to historical and political issues without in any
way qualifying his earlier account, I will argue from the premiss
that Kant's account of the basic structural elements of this faculty
in sections 61–78 apply to teleological judgment in its political
employment.

The concept of a purpose of nature applies to complex systems in
nature which exhibit a form of causality which determines both the
relation of parts to the whole and the relation of the whole to its
parts. Thus, for example, while the leaves of a tree are produced by
the tree, and are only possible in light of the idea of the form of a
tree as a whole, the growth of the tree is caused by the leaves (CJ
371–2, see 370–6). The entire entity is dependent, for its existence,
upon the causality of complex subordinate parts which are systems
in themselves. The parts are complex causal agents in themselves,
but are only possible in light of the idea of the form of the whole.[18]

Kant argues that we cannot achieve a transparent account of
such reciprocal causality through reasoning resting on mechanistic
principles (CJ 369). The understanding's mechanistic scientific concepts are inadequate to explain this causality: we are familiar with

---

[18] The parts are thus 'reciprocally cause and effect of their form' (CJ 373, see 408,
415).

no causality in experience analogous to such a purposive relation (CJ 375).

Kant rejects mechanistic explanations of manifestations of reciprocal causality in complex objects in nature because 'the inner possibility of a whole as a purpose always presupposes that there is an idea of this whole and presupposes that what [the] parts are like depends on that idea' (CJ 408). Thus, Kant considers that it is absurd to hope that 'another Newton might arise who would explain to us, in terms of natural laws unordered by the idea of any intention, how even a mere blade of grass is produced' (CJ 400, see 409). Kant's objection would appear to apply to evolutionary accounts postdating his work, since even evolutionary theory requires the notion of an evolving organism as a starting-point.

Kant asserts that mechanistic explanations provide, at best, a potentially endless regress of causal relations. While we can always extend the explanatory regress an additional step back, such extensions do not offer the information required for explanatory transparency. The question is not simply how complex organisms can be generated, but why such organisms exist at all. Mechanistic accounts explain neither 'why people have to exist' (CJ 378), nor why organisms in general have to exist.

Reason requires 'that even the particular laws of nature be combined in a unified and hence lawful way' (CJ 404). Kant has argued that such systematicity is a necessary presupposition of all scientific investigations of the objects and relations in experience. Yet, such a unified account is undermined when the understanding lacks a pure concept of the understanding to subsume some particular object in nature.

Since no such concept of the understanding can subsume a complex system exhibiting reciprocal causality, reason must supply a subjective principle of purposiveness (defined as 'lawfulness of the contingent') capable of subsuming contingent particular objects (CJ 404). One such purposive principle is the concept of a purpose of nature, which '[helps us] merely to apply understanding generally to objects of possible experience'[19] (CJ 405).

This concept allows us to presuppose, reflectively, that the idea of the whole could be the cause of the parts of the whole (both their

---

[19] 'The concept of a thing as a natural purpose is one that subsumes nature under a causality that is conceivable only [as exercised] by reason' (CJ 396).

existence and their form). Such a concept of reason, applied by the faculty of judgment, enables the understanding to subsume the notion of a system manifesting reciprocal causality under the reflective concept of a purpose of nature. Thus, the concept of a purpose of nature grounds the employment of teleological judgment to determine a lawlike system capable of subsuming and ordering contingent particulars in experience.[20]

In spite of the fact that the concept of a purpose of nature is merely reflective, Kant argues that the concept is 'necessary for human judgment'. Therefore, the concept, as a subjective principle which reason provides to our faculty of judgment, 'holds just as necessarily for our *human judgment* as it would if it were an objective principle' (CJ 404). Teleological judgments grounded in the notion of a purpose of nature therefore *hold necessarily for human judgment.*

The purposiveness exhibited by a purpose of nature is determined by judgment according to concepts.[21] Yet such purposiveness, like the 'objective purposiveness' exhibited by certain geometric figures (CJ 362), appears to be merely formal. The judgment that a complex system is a natural purpose simply determines that the system *is* a purpose; no determination is made of the content of that purpose. The purposiveness seems to be simply 'a suitability for all sorts of purposes (of infinite diversity)' (CJ 366).

The concept of a purpose of nature is a principle of reason, whose 'ultimate demand [for principles] aims at the unconditioned' (CJ 401). Since the purposiveness of a purpose of nature is not necessarily constrained by any law, Kant predictably examines the possibility of an unconditioned natural purpose: a 'suitability for all sort of purposes' unconditioned by any empirical constraints.

If an ultimate purpose of nature can be identified in experience, that object should exhibit unconditioned suitability for purposes.

---

[20] Since mechanical explanation will 'always be inadequate' to provide a systematic account of purposes of nature, 'we are authorized to adopt the following procedure . . . we are to explain all products and events of nature, even the most purposive ones, in mechanical terms as far as we possibly can; . . . [yet] as regards those natural products that we cannot even begin to investigate except under the concept of a purpose of reason, the essential character of our reason will still force us to subordinate such products ultimately, regardless of those mechanical causes, to causality in terms of purposes' (CJ 415).

[21] That is, the judgment that the object is purposive is determined by reasoning according to concepts, rather than by pleasure occasioned by the harmony of our faculties of judgment, as in a judgment of taste.

Since Kant defines 'humanity' as 'the capacity to propose an end to oneself' (DV 392), or unconstrained purposiveness, man, as the embodiment of this quality, is by definition an ultimate end of nature. In addition, man is the only ultimate end of nature: 'man is the ultimate purpose of creation here on earth, because he is the only being on earth who can form a concept of purposes and use his reason to turn an aggregate of purposively structured things into a system of purposes' (CJ 426–7).

Since humanity constitutes the ultimate purpose of nature, humanity must also be considered 'the purpose by reference to which all other natural things constitute a system of purposes' (CJ 429). Thus, the argument developed in connection with the concept of a purpose of nature grounds not merely the notion of a possible lawlike system of purposes in nature, but a substantive account of the highest value orienting such a system. The concept of humanity, as the ultimate purpose of nature, grounds an account of a unified system subsuming and ordering contingent particulars in experience. The specific content of such a system can be exhibited only if judgment can represent the implications of the notion of humanity as an ultimate purpose; but the notion of humanity as an ultimate purpose, by providing a ground for a systematic logic of subsumption in experience, provides the essential foundation for a faculty of judgment capable of specifying these implications.

It is essential to Kant's account of political judgment that this highest value in nature constitutes a moral concept. Even the most compelling account of nature as purposively organized would not, in itself, ground normative judgments. It is precisely 'dependence [of the will] upon natural laws' (CPr 33) that Kant attacks in his critique of hedonic principles of legislation. If reflective political judgment exhibits the substantive implication of a moral principle, however, these implications will ground obligations for all rational beings.

Finally, Kant provides a hint of the political implications of his analysis by examining what purpose, within man himself, is to be furthered through man's connection with nature (CJ 429). Since man is an ultimate purpose of nature *because* of his unique ability to form a 'concept of purposes', it is not surprising that 'man's aptitude in general for setting himself purposes, and for using nature . . . as a means [for achieving them]', his unconditioned suitability for purposes, constitutes the quality 'within man himself, that is a purpose and that he is to further through his connection with nature' (CJ 429–30).

Culture constitutes the means for developing this aptitude in man. Thus, culture, of a specific type, is the ultimate purpose that we 'attribute to nature with respect to the human species' (CJ 431). Only a culture 'adequate to assist the will in the determination and selection of its purposes' can constitute this ultimate purpose. A conception of culture adequate to satisfy this requirement must liberate 'the will from the despotism of desires, a despotism that . . . renders us unable to do our own selecting' (CJ 432).

It is important to note the limits of this move in Kant's argument. The teleological argument merely specifies humanity as the form of purposiveness which constitutes the unconditioned completion of the series of determinations under the concept of a purpose of nature. This argument does not provide a separate basis for respect for freedom, nor a second derivation of the moral requirement to respect humanity. The implications of this conclusion are cognitive, not normative: the possibility of specifying a complete systematic ordering of purposes in nature satisfies a necessary condition for the coherent employment of the understanding.

While the identification of humanity as the 'highest point in the chain of purposes' (CJ 390) has significant implications for the political extension of Kant's teleological argument, the ranking of objects and relations in experience constitutes merely the first of the two operations of reflective judgment. In order to interpret the moral salience of an object or relation in experience, political judgment must not merely characterize the moral relevance of that object, but must also determine the practical implications of that characterization.

As I will argue in Chapter 5, the second operation (interpretation) is accomplished through the symbolic exhibition of the object or relation. Teleological judgment 'exhibits' each purposive concept associated with the form of an object or relation in experience by comparing the concept with an idealized conception of the object or relation 'as it is [meant] to be' (FI 240). The exhibition thus specifies an instantiation of the concept which would realize a higher order of purposiveness.

The specification of 'humanity' as the highest point in the chain of natural purposes locates this moral notion centrally in the orientation of our understanding within the systematic order of nature.

More significantly, however, this specification identifies a fundamental moral concept as one whose exhibition has overriding significance for the structuring of relations in experience.

Since the exhibition of the concept of humanity would reveal practical implications of the unconditioned realization of this moral concept, teleological judgment provides a link between concepts of reason and experience, grounding a direct exhibition of the empirical implications of the moral law. Thus, teleological judgment supplies a basis for judgments realizing the political implications of pure moral concepts. If the moral notion of humanity is located *within* an ordered system with a specifiable logic, even finite human reason may hope to identify its specific substantive implications for relations in experience.

Moreover, while 'humanity' is the highest point in the purposive series 'within nature', it is not the final point in the series of determinations under this concept, since we can still conceive of a form of purposiveness totally unconditioned by any empirical conditions that would constitute the purpose *of the existence of* nature. Thus, exhibition of the notion of 'humanity' (to reveal a higher order of unconditioned purposiveness) will exhibit the purpose which nature, itself, is organized to further (the 'final purpose of creation', CJ 449 n.). Reflective judgments hold necessarily for human reason; every rational human would therefore judge that the purpose of nature was to further the purpose revealed by this exhibition.

Since human agents do not necessarily act on their rational judgments, however, such a judgment would not necessarily motivate any agent to act to further this purpose. The exhibition of this final purpose would, nevertheless, exhibit the practical implications of a fundamental moral concept. Therefore, every moral agent, qua moral agent, would be obligated to further this purpose. Thus, reflective judgment would secure a necessary judgment that the specified end was the end of nature itself, and moral judgment would ground an obligation to further this end.

While the substantive implications of this notion will be developed more fully in the discussion of symbolic presentation in Chapter 5, it seems clear that man's ultimate purpose in nature must be to further the development in man, himself, of a will which is both: (i) free, and (ii) skilled in the formation and pursuit of its own ends. This purpose is both: (i) the highest principle in the systematic account of nature which reason requires us to construct; and (ii) the highest normative and practical principle of morality.

Therefore, it seems that, barring some powerful countervailing consideration, reason should endorse the judgment that we must further norms and institutions which advance the realization of our free ability to form and pursue ends. If certain forms of social relations are inhospitable to the development of such a free pur-posiveness, then we must judge reflectively that the form of such social relations is inconsistent with the purpose that reason necessarily requires that we pursue. In order to generate a political obligation to realize these conditions, however, it will be necessary to argue that rational beings are obligated to realize the institutions that they judge to realize this purpose of reason most fully. I will argue for this claim in Chapter 5.

The complexity and obscurity of Kant's argument in the 'Methodology' have misled even the most subtle commentators. Guyer (1991), for example, argues that Kant's teleological examination of systematicity culminates with the claim that 'the only thing which can be conceived at least by us as a goal and yet is also uncondi-tioned is *our own freedom* . . . the very condition of the possibility of conceiving of the lawfulness of nature . . . drives us to a recogni-tion of our own freedom' (164). Thus, Guyer asserts, the teleologi-cal argument appears to constitute a separate argument both grounding and motivating 'the fundamental principle of morality' (165). These claims are puzzling because the teleological argument does not demonstrate or prove the unconditioned quality of free-dom as a moral quality. Rather, the argument appeals to this qual-ity as something established in the moral philosophy.

Thus, the incorporation of this moral concept in the teleological argument constitutes not a second grounding for the fundamental moral principle, but rather a convergence of two separate lines of argument. Kant's moral philosophy argues for the unconditioned status of freedom. The teleological argument attempts to demon-strate that relations in experience in fact constitute a lawfully or-dered system. The incorporation of the fundamental moral concept as a central element of the teleological argument grounds an addi-tional claim: a central moral concept plays a fundamental role in structuring the systematic order of relations in experience.

Moreover, the goal specified by teleological judgment is not, as Guyer asserts, freedom; rather, it is 'man as a moral subject'

(CJ 435) or 'man under moral laws' (CJ 445). Kant's specification of a realizable state of affairs, rather than a mere idea, as the final goal reflects the transformation of his teleological argument from an argument for rational faith to an argument for morally oriented political judgment. By identifying a fundamental moral concept (humanity) as a key element in the analysis specifying the systematic order which characterizes relations in experience, Kant is able to articulate systematic implications of this moral concept for empirical relations in experience.

Unlike Guyer, Makkreel (1990) stresses the interaction of moral and teleological judgment in his examination of Kant's teleological argument. Thus, Makkreel argues that moral self-understanding requires that human reason 'supplement the determinant principles of [practical] reason with the reflective principle of judgment', in order to 'interpret history from a moral perspective' (168). Yet because Makkreel understands reflective judgment as merely 'supplementing' practical reason, reflective interpretation of history, in his interpretation, must constitute merely an 'indirect appropriation of the moral insights of reason' (169). Thus, reflective judgments hold contingently, rather than necessarily, and 'must also rely on experiential intimations of progress and aesthetic symbols of hope for its orientation' (169).

Yet, if my argument is correct, reflective political judgments hold necessarily for human judgment, and ground moral obligations. As reflective judgments, they hold necessarily for human reason; and as exhibitions specifying the substantive implications of a fundamental moral concept, they ground obligations for all moral agents.

Such an account of the significance, for relations in experience, of teleological judgment might appear too unrestrictedly speculative to fit comfortably within Kant's critical project. What constraints prevent wildly speculative applications of this line of reasoning?

Teleological judgment is constrained in two senses. First, Kant narrowly constrains the cases in which we are authorized to assign a purposive principle to an object as the basis for an extrinsic teleological judgment. 'Only in one case' within experience are we justified in the determination that an object is a purpose of nature and thus manifests external purposiveness (CJ 366–8). The formal condition under which we can apply the concept of external purposiveness is that we perceive a relation of cause and effect that we can see as law-governed only if we see the cause's action as based on the effect (CJ 366).

Kant asserts that this condition is met only in the case of particular forms of organized entities.[22] An organized being instantiates Kant's condition in the sense that the purposive activity of the parts can only be explained in terms of the idea of the whole entity. If the constituent parts of an organized system (i.e. heart, lung) are viewed as causes of the existence of the system (i.e. a healthy animal), then we can see the relation of cause (organ) to whole (animal) as law-governed only if we see the cause's action (function of the lung) as based on the effect (contributing to the health of the animal). We obtain a coherent picture of the relation of parts to whole only if we begin from the idea of the whole.

Yet organization of the parts under the idea of the whole is a necessary, rather than sufficient, condition for identifying a purpose of nature. Kant specifies two conditions under which we are authorized to consider a thing to be a purpose of nature. First, both the possibility of the existence and the form of the parts 'must depend on their relation to the whole' (CJ 373). Second, the parts must combine to cause the whole 'because they are reciprocally cause and effect of their form' (CJ 373). The first condition, without the second, characterizes 'merely a work of art': the object is 'then the product of a rational cause distinct from the matter of the thing' (CJ 373). Only when both conditions characterize the object does the mutual dependence of parts and whole determine a purpose of nature.

Kant constrains teleological judgment in a second sense by restricting it to a specific, non-constitutive use: the idea of the whole is not understood as *causing* the relation of whole to parts. Rather, it must be necessary to conceive of the idea of the whole as the only 'basis on which someone judging this whole cognizes the systematic unity in the form and combination of all the manifold contained in the given matter' (CJ 373). Thus, teleological judgment is not intended to establish truth claims, but to provide the kind of systematic explanation required to render nature transpar-

---

[22] 'Only insofar as matter is organized does it necessarily carry with it the concept of it as a natural purpose' (CJ 378).

ent to reason.[23] In teleological judgment, we 'bring nature under principles of observation and investigation by *analogy* with the causality in terms of purposes' (CJ 360, see 375). The necessary transparency can be approximated by identifying an underlying purposive principle which can be placed in a systematic ordering of principles of nature.

Thus, suitably constrained in its employment and interpretation, teleological judgment provides a law-governed order of objects in nature by referring objects to an already given determining purposive principle (see CJ 379). Teleological judgment thus appears to provide a general methodology for the systematic ordering of objects and relations in experience in the service of explanatory transparency: 'once we have discovered that nature is able to make products that can be thought of only in terms of the concept of final causes, we are then entitled to go further: we may thereupon judge products as belonging to a system of purposes' (CJ 380).

CONCLUSION

A Kantian political theory requires an account of moral salience to bridge the gulf between pure principles and experience, and thus to exhibit the substantive implications of the metaphysical principles of right for positive legislation. Kant's argument for the necessary systematicity of nature and experience offers a viable basis for linking principles to experience. Moreover, the analysis of a purpose of nature, as constrained by Kant's account of the nature of human reason, necessarily culminates in an ultimate moral purpose. Thus, Kant's account of systematicity in the *Critique of Judgment* appears well suited to ground an account of moral salience.

If rules of moral salience play a central role in Kant's politics, however, political judgment may not require the full determination of a system of objective ends. A faculty of judgment which (i) characterizes objects in experience and (ii) specifies the significance of such objects, in itself mediates between pure principles and experience without the aid of a heuristic ideal criterion. If reflective

---

[23] 'We settle for regarding natural purposes as objects that are *explicable* solely in terms of natural laws that must be conceived of by using the idea of purposes as principle' (CJ 383).

judgment is capable of mediating directly between pure principles and objects in experience, then, while Kant's focus on the notion of a system of objective ends would indicate the kind of interest Kant wants to identify (the social commitment of a rational being, qua rational being) and its modality (necessity), the representation of a system of objective ends might not be a necessary step in forming the judgment.

5

Political Judgment

IN Chapter 4, I argue that Kant's account of systematicity, in the *Critique of Judgment*, does in fact ground judgments regarding the moral salience of objects in experience. Kant's account of systematicity, however, grounds teleological *interpretation* of experience without necessarily grounding practical judgments. In order to constitute a basis for practical judgment, teleological judgment must subordinate the teleological *interpretation* of experience to an account of the necessary commitments of a rational subject.

Kant argues that it is possible to judge reflectively that (i) the form of an object of experience embodies a purposive concept;[1] and (ii) such a purposive concept is embedded in an ordered system of purposes of nature.[2] Therefore, it might seem that reflective judgment should provide a decisive input to an agent's practical deliberations regarding objects and their relations in experience. Reflectively, we can identify the ultimate end of nature and the principles governing the subsumption of other forms of purposiveness to that end. Therefore, in our relation to objects in experience, we should act to further purposes which advance the

[1] We present the purposiveness of the object 'on an objective basis: as the harmony of the form of the object with the possibility of the thing itself according to a prior concept of the thing itself that contains the basis of that form' (CJ 192). Teleological judgments 'connect with the presentation of an object a determinate concept of a purpose and regard the possibility of the object as based on that concept ... our judging of the object's possibility is based on a concept (of a purpose) that precedes a priori [that possibility]' (FI 239–40).

[2] The concept that an object is a natural purpose 'on account of its intrinsic form ... leads us necessarily to the idea of all of nature as a system in terms of the rule of purposes' (CJ 378–9). '[T]his principle [for judging nature teleologically] ... serves us as a guide that allows us to consider natural things in terms of a new law-governed order by referring them to an already given basis [a purpose] as that which determines them' (CJ 379). '[W]e are then entitled to go further; we may thereupon judge products as belonging to a system of purposes even if they ... do not require us ... to look for a different principle beyond the mechanism of blind efficient causes' (CJ 380–1).

realization of the ultimate end of nature, or failing that, the highest-order subsidiary end which it is possible to further. Thus, reflective judgment should determine the significance of the purposiveness manifest in empirical objects for our practical deliberations.

In fact, the judgment that an object's form embodies a purposive concept is a necessary, rather than sufficient, condition for determining the significance of such an object for practical reason. Such a judgment provides merely the *basis* for a further judgment regarding the practical significance of such an empirical object. For example, the judgment that a tree embodies a higher order of purposiveness than a watch (because the elements of the tree, unlike those of the watch, 'are reciprocally the cause and effect of their form' (CJ 373) contributes to the specification of the systematicity of nature, but provides no ground for a maxim of action. The higher-order status of the tree, in itself, does not alter the agent's process for evaluating his subjective maxims of action.

At this point in Kant's argument, the systematic order of nature is not specified in a way which necessarily grounds practical judgments. The logic of Kant's argument grounds the judgment that man's capability for purposes is the ultimate end of nature, and that a culture of discipline will further this ability more effectively than a culture of skill. Yet this judgment provides (i) a principled basis for interpreting history as consistent with moral progress, rather than (ii) a ground for a potential maxim of action. As such, the judgment is not practical.

The identification of the form of an empirical object with an underlying purposive concept merely constitutes the precondition for a teleological judgment. The judgment itself involves the comparison of the purposive concept of the object with a concept of 'what [the object] is [meant] to be' (FI 240). We must derive an ideal concept from the purposive concept instantiated by the object, and use this second notion as a criterion to evaluate the first concept (that is, the purposive concept implicit in the form of the object).

Through this procedure, Kant believes, teleological judgment can generate normative claims grounded in the systematic purposiveness of nature. We necessarily judge that an object is 'meant' to be realized in a way which is incompletely reflected in its current condition; this judgment reflects an orientation towards nature which we hold necessarily as rational creatures. Therefore, in acting rationally, we ought to act on a maxim of furthering the object's more completely realized state.

In this chapter, I will examine: (i) the methodology of teleological judgment; (ii) the political significance of Kant's political teleology; and (iii) the intersubjective quality of the judgment.

1. METHODOLOGY

In teleological reflection on the purposive concept associated with an object, judgment: (i) derives, from the purposive concept implicit in the form of the object, 'a prior concept of the thing that contains the basis of that form'[3] (CJ 192); (ii) compares this derived concept to the purposive concept implicit in the object's form; and (iii) applies conclusions arising from this comparison to the object.

Several aspects of this account are problematic. First, how does one form a concept 'that contains the basis for [the object's] form'? Second, what kind of comparison is appropriate between purposive concepts; and why should the results of such a comparison have normative implications for our relations to objects in experience? Finally, how do we apply the results of a conceptual comparison to an object or relation in experience?

In order to derive an ideal concept of the object, we need to (i) exhibit the salient aspects of the object's purposive concept, and (ii) develop their substantive implications. In the 'Methodology of Teleological Judgment', Kant employs such an approach to derive an ideal concept (the concept of a final purpose of creation) from the concept of an object as it exists in nature (the concept of autonomous humanity as the ultimate purpose of nature).

Kant's account of his methodology, however, is curiously episodic. Kant first presents a sketch of the method of symbolic exhibition (CJ 351 ff.), and describes the method as 'deserv[ing] fuller investigation', but not at that point in the text (the discussion of 'Beauty as the Symbol of Morality').[4] Kant then employs this method in the argument identifying a final purpose of creation

---

[3] Or, analogously, judgment determines a concept of 'what [the object] is [meant] to be' (FI 240).

[4] 'This function [of judgment] has not been analyzed much so far, even though it very much deserves fuller investigation; but this is not the place to pursue it' (CJ 352).

(CJ 434 ff.). The method relies heavily on inference by analogy; yet Kant has neither (i) discussed the warrant for employing analogical reasoning in practical judgment, nor (ii) described the constraints under which analogical reasoning is properly employed. Finally, almost as an afterthought, Kant explains his reliance on inference by analogy, and describes the conditions under which analogical reasoning can be reliably employed (CJ 464–5).

In order to clarify Kant's logic, I will deviate from his order of presentation. First, I will discuss the methodology Kant describes in his discussion of 'symbolic exhibition'. Second, I will present and evaluate Kant's arguments for the use of analogical reasoning in judgment. Finally, I will examine Kant's use of this method in the argument identifying a final purpose of creation.

A. *Symbolic Exhibition*

Symbolic exhibition '[serves] as a means for reproducing concepts in accordance with the imagination's law of association' (CJ 352). The method is employed to exhibit concepts of reason 'to which no sensible intuition can be adequate' (CJ 351).

In the symbolic exhibition of a concept, judgment 'applies' the concept to a sensible intuition to which we have reflectively related the concept by analogy. Judgment then reflects upon the intuition in light of the concept, and finally applies the 'mere rule by which it reflects on that intuition' to 'an entirely different object, of which the former is only the symbol'.[5]

While this account is suggestive, it is also ambiguous. What is the relation between the initial concept and the 'analogous' sensible object? How is the symbolic object selected, and what is its relation to the initial sensible object? How are we to specify the 'mere rule' of reflection? Kant's description of symbolic exhibition is only a sketch, and it must be read together with his comments on examples and related issues in order to present anything resembling a workable method.

Kant provides two examples in which one object symbolically represents another: (i) a constitutional monarchy may be presented

---

[5] 'Symbolic exhibition [of a concept of reason] uses an analogy (for which we use empirical intuitions as well), in which judgment performs a double function: it applies the concept to the object of a sensible intuition; and then it applies the mere rule by which it reflects on that intuition to an entirely different object, of which the former is only the symbol' (CJ 352).

as an animate body; (ii) an absolute dictatorship may be presented as a mere machine. The relevance of these examples to Kant's account of symbolic exhibition is initially obscure, because Kant fails to indicate the concept the objects are to exhibit. All of the sensible objects mentioned (a monarchy,[6] a machine, an animate body), however, are complex systems in which 'the possibility of its parts (as concerns both their existence and their form) [depends] on their relation to the whole' (CJ 373). Thus, Kant's examples all satisfy the first of Kant's two requirements for the specification of a purpose of nature.

An object in nature exhibiting such purposiveness but not reciprocal causation between the parts and the whole (the second requirement), however, is 'merely a work of art' (CJ 373). Thus, the degree to which the objects satisfy the second requirement distinguishes works of art (artifice), such as a watch, from purposes of nature. Objects which satisfy both requirements can be further distinguished by the degree to which the purposiveness manifested is unconditioned.

The examples of complex systems which Kant employs as symbolic representations (an animate body, a machine) therefore constitute archetypes which can be ranked by: (i) form of purposiveness (artistic or natural); (ii) degree to which the purposiveness is unconditioned. Such a ranking provides the basis for a scale of organized purposiveness in nature. Each potential exhibition of a given concept can thus be ranked according to the degree to which the object of the exhibition approaches unconditioned purposiveness. An animate body therefore exhibits a higher form of purposiveness, on Kant's scale, than a machine.

Thus, by (i) comparing the concept of an organized being, by analogical reasoning, to forms of political organization; and (ii) representing different forms of regime by archetypes of organized beings presenting different degrees of purposiveness, Kant provides a basis for deriving from the concept of a merely artistic form of purposiveness in political organization (a tyranny) the concept of 'what it is [meant] to be', that is an unconditionally

---

[6] Kant does not explicitly describe a monarchy as a complex system in nature. Moreover, much of Kant's discussion of teleological judgments regarding complex systems deals with discrete natural entities, rather than forms of social organization. Kant's later discussion of the body politic as a natural purpose, however, indicates that Kant interpreted political units as a kind of complex system in nature.

purposive realization of this form of complex system (a constitutional monarchy).

Generally, judgment identifies a purposive concept implicit in the form of a given object, and specifies a formal characteristic of the purposive concept (e.g. the possibility of the parts depends on their relation to the whole) which applies identically to the concept and to a second empirical object. The concept is presented symbolically by this second empirical object, which is identical to the concept in terms of the formal characteristic, but which is merely one member of a hierarchy of empirical objects representing different degrees of realization of the purposive concept. Finally, judgment reflects on the rule of reflection governing the hierarchy. This reflection locates the initial object in the hierarchy determined in nature by the purposive concept; a comparison of the symbolic presentation of the concept (the second empirical object) with other objects in the hierarchy grounds a reflective judgment determining the most complete realization of the initial object.

In order to understand Kant's employment of analogical reasoning in teleological judgment, we need an account of (i) the warrant for critical employment of analogical reasoning and (ii) the necessary conditions for its proper employment. Before examining Kant's account of analogical reasoning, however, I will note two potential objections to this account of the role of symbolic presentation in reflective judgment.

First, Kant's only explicit discussion of symbolic presentation is presented in a discussion of aesthetic, not teleological judgment. While Kant's discussion *is* physically located in the *Critique of Aesthetic Judgment*, however, Kant is careful to indicate that the discussion of symbolic presentation is *not* limited to applications in that particular context: 'This function [of judgment] has not been analyzed much so far, even though it very much deserves fuller investigation; but this is not the place to pursue it' (CJ 352). Moreover, Kant appears committed to the claim that exhibition for teleological judgment *must* be symbolic. He claims that *all* exhibition must be schematic or symbolic. Schematic exhibition applies only to concepts of the understanding, while the purposive concepts of teleological judgment are concepts of reason. Therefore, the concepts of teleological judgment can *only* be exhibited symbolically. Finally, the examples of symbolic exhibition which Kant offers (constitutional monarchy; absolute dictatorship) have no tangible relation to aesthetic judgment.

Second, it can be argued that no exhibition of the purposive concept of a natural purpose is necessary: the object which we have judged to be a natural purpose *is* the exhibition. This is technically true. An exhibition 'place[s] beside the concept an intuition corresponding to it' (CJ 192–3). The empirical object prompting our reflection on natural purposiveness *is* the intuition corresponding to our concept of a natural purpose.[7] The concept of natural purpose is not, however, a concept of the object, but 'only a principle of judgment by which it provides itself with concepts in nature's immense diversity (so that judgment can orient itself in this diversity)' (CJ 193). The empirical object which prompts the reflection leads us to the concept, but the concept is not limited to the object. It is relevant to note that symbolic exhibition is appropriate where no empirical intuition is 'adequate' to the concept in question (CJ 351).

In fact, since Kant seems committed to the position that the exhibition of concepts of reason must be symbolic, an empirical object *cannot* constitute the exhibition of the concept of a natural purpose: symbolic presentations 'contain nothing whatever that belongs to the intuition of the object; their point is the subjective one of serving as a means for reproducing concepts in accordance with the imagination's law of association' (CJ 352).

In 'What is Orientation in Thinking', Kant appears to endorse this account of reason's employment of analogical reasoning in its self-orientation. When reason 'seeks to extend its sphere beyond the frontiers of experience and no longer encounters any objects of intuition whatsoever', reason 'reduce[s] at least the *relationship* between the [merely intelligible] object in question and objects of experience to pure concepts of the understanding'. Through this process, we 'think of something which is itself supra-sensory as capable of being applied by our reason to the world of experience' (WOT 240).

B. Inference by Analogy

Analogical reasoning plays a prominent role in Kant's account of teleological judgment. In particular, this approach is employed in both the account of symbolic exhibition and the argument iden-

---

[7] In fact, Kant states that we 'may regard *natural purposes* as the exhibition of the concept of a real (objective) purposiveness' (CJ 193).

tifying final purposes in nature. Yet Kant has offered no account of the method of analogical reasoning or defence of its validity.

In fact, such a method of reasoning appears to invite the transcendent illusion of traditional metaphysics. As noted in Chapter 4, Kant held that the traditional error was to take the conditioned as a thing in itself, rather than an appearance (A499/B527). Reflective judgment was to avoid such an error by taking only the form, but not the matter, of conditioned empirical objects as given.

Thus, Kant's account of inference by analogy involves the consideration of the merely formal aspects of objects: '*Analogy* . . . is the identity of the relation between bases and consequences insofar as it is present despite what difference in kind there is between the things themselves' (CJ 464 n.). Analogy provides a reliable basis for inference only when the 'basis' on which we draw our inference is 'the same' in the two objects compared (when 'we do have *par ratio* [the same grounds]'). By abstracting away from the substantive and focusing on the purely formal aspects, the method avoids the danger of illusion. In addition, by limiting inferences to cases in which the formal aspect which grounds the judgment is identically present in both objects, the method ensures that the grounds of the judgment are the same for both objects.

Objects and relations in experience are not ordered by a priori principles; thus, Kant's account of the systematicity of nature requires some methodology for generating principles which are to govern such a lawlike system. Since inference by analogy is a necessary condition for the possibility of systematicity of nature (which is itself a necessary condition of cognition), such inferences are objective if they are properly grounded. Inference by analogy thus features prominently in Kant's teleological theory because the systematicity of nature can only be specified for human understanding through the employment of such inferences.

C. Symbol, Analogy, and Final Purposes

Symbolic exhibition provides a method for applying analogical reasoning to the fundamental problem of teleological judgment: specification of a systematic purposive relationship holding, at least for human judgment, between objects in experience. Exhibition provides the basis for locating objects and relations in experience within an ordering structured by the systematic logic of purposes which reason necessarily judges to characterize objects in nature. Exhibition therefore defines a range of relations between empirical objects over which an exhibited concept extends. Once this range is specified, the relations between the objects in this range can be determined by reflecting on the nature of the complex organization that they manifest. In identifying and ordering a range of objects in experience, reflective judgment defines the concept's role in specifying the systematic order of objects in experience.

Kant's argument for humanity as the ultimate purpose of nature (discussed in Chapter 4) provides a good example of Kant's use of symbolic exhibition in his examination of the systematicity of nature. Kant begins with the concept of a purpose of nature (which judgment requires to account for the causality we encounter in complex natural objects). It is specifically the task of teleological judgment to provide an account of the purposiveness characterizing relations among complex systems in nature; thus, the notion of a complex object as a purpose of nature provides the basic unit of analysis for teleological judgment.

Kant considers objects to which this concept applies in nature: self-organized beings (e.g. organic entities). The common quality exhibited by such objects is a suitability for purposes: even the most primitive organic units aim at their own nourishment and reproduction. Thus, such suitability for purposes provides the ground for analogical extension of the concept.

Since the highest-order principle for teleological judgment must ground 'the connection in terms of purposes of the world', an ultimate purpose of nature (as determinable by human reason) must be a purpose 'by reference to which all other natural things constitute a system of purposes' (CJ 429). Therefore, reason requires a highest-order principle of the greatest generality. The most general principle associated with a suitability for purposes within nature must be 'man's aptitude in general for setting himself purposes' (CJ 431). Therefore, organisms embodying such generalized purposiveness (mankind in general) are specified as the ultimate purpose of nature.

Thus, judgment reflectively identifies: (i) the quality which grounds the system of purposes in nature (for reason); and (ii) the empirical object which embodies this quality. Kant begins by applying the concept of a purpose of nature to objects in nature, and then proceeds to identify a *basis* in these objects (suitability for purposes) to ground an analogy with a second set of objects which exemplify such purposiveness generally, unconditioned by any reference to other purposes. This employment of analogical reasoning permits the specification of a unique ultimate purpose: only rational beings exhibit highest-order suitability for purposes.

It is relevant to note that Kant's earlier argument (for an ordering of organized beings distinguishing and ranking complex systems according to the purposive principle implicit in their form) is essential for orienting the analysis. Only with respect to such an ordering can judgment conclude that the form of organized being which demonstrates the highest order of self-organization constitutes a standard for the lower-order forms.

Kant applies the same form of reasoning to the argument for 'man under moral law' as the final purpose of creation. A final purpose is a purpose 'that requires no other purpose as a condition of its possibility' (CJ 434). Kant argues that, 'if we assume that the connection in terms of possibility in the world is real' (as we must qua rational being, since teleological judgment holds necessarily for human reason), then the determination of the ends which objects serve *in nature* is merely an additional conditioned determination (in the series of determinations grounded in the concept of purposes).

Since reason requires an unconditioned determination for every series of conditioned determinations, reason requires that each sequence of determinations exhibiting the structure that a purposive concept imposes on nature must culminate in an unconditioned determination. If judgment determines that organized beings 'have the form they have' for the sake of some end of nature (CJ 434), the determination remains conditioned upon the existence of purposes in nature. An unconditioned final determination must specify the 'objective basis' for the existence of purposes in nature, per se (independent of other purposes or objects in nature).[8] Such an objective basis is a purpose *of the existence of*

---

[8] If 'we find in the world arrangements in terms of purposes, and we follow reason's inevitable demand to subordinate these merely conditioned purposes to a supreme unconditioned one, i.e. a final purpose, then, to begin with, we are obviously not concerned with a purpose of (i.e. within) nature, so far as nature [already] exists, but with the purpose of the [very] existence of nature and all its arrangements' (CJ 443). Reason requires an account of 'a basis determining [the object] that is not always conditioned in turn . . . [it] must be of such a kind that in the order of purposes, it depends on no condition other than the idea of it (CJ 435).

nature itself, 'to which all of nature is subordinated' (CJ 436 n.), and therefore cannot be grounded in some relation to objects existing *in* nature. Thus, reason requires a concept of purposiveness unconditioned by any aspects of empirical nature (a final purpose).

Thus, the highest-order principle associated with a suitability for purposes in general must be unconditioned purposiveness. Kant's argument extends the notion of unconditioned purposiveness beyond mere abstraction from empirical causation (which merely required that the purposiveness originate independent of mechanistic chains of causes). A final purpose must be a form of purposiveness which is entirely unconditioned. Kant claims that we have knowledge of one unique causality sufficient to determine a purposiveness of this type: 'the moral principle that determines us to action' (CJ 436 n.). Thus, 'man under moral law' must be the final purpose of creation.

As in his investigation of the notion of an ultimate purpose of nature, Kant here applies a purposive concept (in this case the concept of a purpose of nature) to objects (actual purposes of nature), and specifies a basis for the extension of the concept to a more fully realized conception. The basis is general purposiveness, and Kant extends the concept to the furthest point in the sequence of determinations by demanding unconditioned purposiveness of this type. Reasoning from this basis, Kant specifies an object within experience which manifests unconditioned purposiveness, and thus represents the full realization of the concept: man under moral law. In specifying this object, judgment symbolically represents the determinate implications of the underlying moral concept (humanity) for relations in experience.

D. Conclusion: The Method of Teleological Judgment

Teleological judgment involves two discrete, but related, operations. The first, prejudgmental, operation, identifies the purposive concept underlying the form of an organized being in nature. Kant argues that the transcendental necessity of a principle of the systematicity of nature licenses the application of the concept of a purpose of nature to organized objects in nature manifesting reciprocal causality.

The concept of a purpose of nature provides the basic unit of analysis for an understanding of nature as a lawlike system of interrelated purposes. The licence to apply this concept to organized entities in nature warrants the interpretation of events in nature as, in fact, organized to achieve the ends to which nature is teleologically subordinated. Thus, this application of the transcendental principle warrants the judgment that the teleological ends of nature are realizable *within* nature[9] (CJ 444, TPP 108, 112–12, 121–3, CF 85; but see CJ 450).

The second operation associates a concept with a range of objects in experience which can be ordered according to the 'objective purposiveness . . . of the whole of nature' (CJ 380) identified by the first operation of teleological judgment. The second operation grounds normative claims, in a dual sense, by establishing 'man under moral law' as the purpose *of* nature itself. First, as discussed in Chapter 4, this judgment exhibits substantive implications of the fundamental moral concept. Second, such a judgment holds necessarily for human reason: if rational beings, qua rational, necessarily judge that it is the purpose of nature to achieve a specific moral end, then every rational being must judge that he or she ought to realize such an end. This final determination renders the systematicity of nature, and complex forms of life within nature, transparent *for human reason*.

Thus, reflective judgment specifies both the purposive concept underlying an object's form and the logic governing the object's possible evolution or reformulation to realize this underlying concept. In specifying the logic governing the realization of a concept in experience, reflective judgment mediates between concepts and objects in experience exemplifying such concepts. The political application of reflective judgment should therefore make possible a mediation between the principles of natural law and the institutions, legislation, and norms exemplifying those principles in experience.

---

[9] '[The general will as it is given a priori] can also, within the mechanism of nature, be the cause which leads to the intended result and gives effect to the concept of right' (TPP 123). In addition, Kant offers, in support of the claim that 'the human race [is] continually improving', the assertion that interference with such progress is 'a reversal of the *ultimate purpose* of creation' (CF 185). Unlike the 'convulsions which . . . engulfed the animal and vegetable kingdoms', a similar convulsion engulfing human progress would reverse the ultimate purpose of creation; therefore, we must regard it as 'tenable within the most strictly theoretical context' that such progress towards the ultimate purpose will continue.

2. POLITICAL SIGNIFICANCE

While teleological judgment orients practical choice, the exercise of this faculty might not ground the judgment that any particular political institutions are practically necessary. The final purpose of creation, which orients reflective judgment's practical determinations, is specified as 'man under moral laws' (CJ 448 n.). Examination of an alternate formulation, which Kant rejects, suggests the potential of teleological argument to eliminate, rather than enhance, the useful role of political theory within Kantian philosophy.

The basis for the reflective specification of a final purpose of creation is the notion of unconditioned purposiveness. The fullest conception of unconditioned purposiveness might seem to be: 'man *in accordance with* the moral law', since such a formulation requires that man act directly from a pure rational motivation. Yet Kant rejects such a characterization of the final purpose: 'the latter expression would say more than we know . . . [such a view would imply] that we had insight both into the supersensible substrate of nature and into the identity of this substrate with what the causality [that acts] through freedom makes possible in the world' (CJ 449 n.).

It is revealing to consider the implications of this rejected formulation. If the final purpose which orients necessary judgments about objects and relations in experience were a notion of man acting from pure ideas of reason, then the final purpose could only be represented by a direct application of ideas of reason to objects in experience; yet Kant denies that such an application is possible. Reflective judgment is intended to offer an indirect bridge between pure ideas and empirical objects and relations in experience. Yet if the final purpose, the highest-order value which orients all practical reflective judgments, could only be specified through the direct application of a pure idea to objects in experience, the entire argument would merely restate the problematic of the gulf between reason and experience.

It is relevant to note that this is precisely the result in Kant's moral teleology. The required object of a rational will is specified as a pure idea. Since such an idea cannot be realized through any causality known in experience, the necessity of such an object of the will requires the postulate of a divine intelligence securing the final goal required by reason.

Kant avoids this result, in the *Critique of Judgment*, by defining the final purpose of creation as 'man *under* moral laws' (CJ 445, 449 n.). Since we do not have direct knowledge of the supersensible substrate, we cannot realize in nature an objective (man in accordance with moral laws) which requires a supersensible form of causality. Rather, we can only approximate such an objective through symbolic exhibition of the concept of an ultimate purpose of nature. Thus, within the constraints of experience, we can only conceive of a final purpose which instantiates 'man under moral laws'.

This specification provides the condition under which political institutions become necessary. First, if man is 'under' the moral law, then he is not acting purely from moral motivation. Some external incentive is required to motivate, or coerce, compliance with the requirements of the moral law. Political institutions, preeminently, supply this incentive. Kant sketches the outlines of the necessary institutions in the *Critique of Judgment*:

The formal condition under which nature can alone achieve this final aim is that constitution of human relations where the impairment to freedom which results from the mutually conflicting freedom [of individuals] is countered by lawful authority within a whole called *civil society*. For only in this constitution of human relations can our natural predispositions develop maximally. But this constitution requires something further . . . a *cosmopolitan* whole, a system of all states that are in danger of affecting one another detrimentally. (CJ 432)

Thus, reflective judgment determines that political institutions must, at a minimum: (i) guarantee mutual external freedom; and (ii) further the realization of a cosmopolitan whole which will ensure world peace. Each of these general requirements grounds a system of subsidiary requirements. The requirement of mutual external freedom grounds the entire substance of the *Rechtslehre*[10] and 'Theory and Practice',[11] while the requirement of furthering a cosmopolitan whole grounds the moral argument for political

---

[10] 'Right is therefore the sum of the conditions under which the choice of one can be united with the choice of another in accordance with a universal law of freedom . . . "Any action is *right* if it can coexist with everyone's freedom in accordance with a universal law"' (MJ 231).

[11] '*Right* is the restriction of each individual's freedom so that it harmonizes with the freedom of everyone else' (TP 73).

obligation developed in *Towards Perpetual Peace*, and other late essays.

While this passage (CJ 432) describes the necessary conditions for the realization of the *ultimate* (not the final) purpose of nature, the conditions necessary to realize such a 'maximal' development of man's 'natural predispositions' in fact define the final purpose of creation: man under moral law. This coincidence results because the task of sustaining the unconditioned quality of man's purposiveness and the task of respecting man's humanity are, in fact, identical. Our reflective judgment specifying the purpose of nature and our reflective judgment determining our obligation within nature coincide, defining one end which is both obligatory and the ultimate end which reason determines that nature must be organized to further.

It is instructive to note how 'Towards Perpetual Peace' develops the argument in the *Critique of Judgment*. Kant advances two independent claims: (i) '[t]he mechanical process of nature visibly exhibits the purposive plan of producing concord among men' (TPP 108); and (ii) 'it is a *moral task* . . . to bring about perpetual peace . . . as a state of affairs which must arise out of recognizing one's duty' (TPP 122).[12]

As in the *Critique of Judgment*, Kant argues for the necessity of judging that: (i) our observations of events within nature permit the interpretation of nature as a lawful system furthering a(n) (ultimate) purpose; and (ii) we are obligated to further a final purpose of creation (which coincides with the necessary conditions for realization of the ultimate purpose of nature). Reflective judgment determines both: (i) an ultimate purpose towards which all purposes within nature are directed [which structures the system of purposes within nature]; and (ii) an unconditioned obligation to realize a final end which is the purpose of the existence of nature itself.

Kant's claim that perpetual peace can be realized 'within the mechanism of nature' is essential to the validity of an *obligation* to realize perpetual peace: moral aims cannot amount to duties unless it is not 'demonstrably impossible to fulfill them' (TP 89, see TPP 116). Thus, Kant takes some care to argue for the plausibility of

---

[12] '[The general will], if only it is put into practice in a consistent way, can also, within the mechanism of nature, be the cause which . . . gives effect to the concept of right' (TP 123).

interpreting nature as a teleologically organized system of purposes directed towards an ultimate purpose.

Kant's argument for the possibility of achieving the ultimate purpose of nature takes the following form. Kant first notes that 'many maintain that [a republican constitution] would only be possible within a state of *angels*' (TPP 112). In fact, Kant claims, 'nature comes to the aid of the universal and rational human will' in realizing republican government *and* perpetual peace: 'the mechanism of nature can be applied to men in such a manner that the antagonism of their hostile attitudes will make them compel one another to submit to coercive laws, thereby producing a condition of peace within which the laws can be enforced' (TPP 113). Thus, the mechanism of nature 'can be used by reason to facilitate the attainment of its own end, the reign of established right' (TPP 113).

Thus, Kant claims, nature in a sense 'guarantees' the realization of man's moral end[13] (TPP 114). Kant's claim for such a guarantee, here and elsewhere in 'Towards Perpetual Peace', might seem to be of the dogmatic type which he criticizes in the *Critique of Judgment*.[14] Yet, in the same paragraph, Kant asserts that the 'likelihood of [this goal's] being attained is not sufficient to enable us to *prophecy* the future theoretically' (TPP 114). Rather, the likelihood is simply 'enough for practical purposes'. Thus, Kant's claim for the guarantee is, in fact, practical rather than dogmatic.[15] The argument for a 'guarantee' is important because it establishes that perpetual peace is 'more than an empty chimera'; therefore, since the goal is possible, it *is* 'our duty to work our way towards this goal' (TPP 114).

[13] 'In this way, nature guarantees perpetual peace by the actual mechanism of human inclinations' (TPP 114).

[14] '[W]e have no a priori basis whatever for the following presumption: how purposes that are not ours . . . yet are to constitute, a special kind of causality, or at least a quite distinct lawfulness of nature. Not only [do we have no a priori basis for such a presumption,] but even experience cannot prove that there actually are such purposes, unless we do some subtle reasoning, and simply slip the concept of a purpose into the nature of things rather than take it from objects and our empirical cognition of them' (CJ 359).

[15] Kant seems primarily concerned to respond to the claim that perpetual peace and its constituent elements can only be achieved in 'a state of angels'. Kant's real concern is to establish that furthering perpetual peace is possible, rather than certain: 'A problem of this kind must be soluble . . . it only means finding out how the mechanism of nature can be applied to men in such a manner that the antagonism of their hostile attitudes will make them compel one another to submit to coercive laws, thereby producing a condition of peace within which the laws can be enforced' (TPP 113).

It is important not to conflate Kant's argument for a guarantee within nature with his argument for a moral obligation to further perpetual peace: 'if I say that nature *wills* that this or that should happen, this does not mean that nature imposes on us a *duty* to do it, for duties can only be imposed by practical reason, acting without any external constraint' (TPP 112). In fact, Kant asserts, it is 'our duty to promote [perpetual peace] *by using* the natural mechanism' (TPP 109, emphasis mine).

Thus, reflective judgment specifies both the purpose of civil society (realizing 'man under moral laws') and the logic governing the possible evolution or reformulation of a society to realize this underlying concept (approximation of such an objective through symbolic exhibition of the concept of an ultimate purpose of nature). The political application of reflective judgment therefore makes possible a mediation between the principles of natural law and the institutions, legislation, and norms exemplifying those principles in experience.

3. UNITY OF REFLECTIVE JUDGMENT: THE *SENSUS COMMUNIS* AND THE INTERSUBJECTIVITY OF TELEOLOGICAL JUDGMENT

The argument presented in sections 1 and 2 suggests that reflective judgment grounds judgments regarding empirical objects in experience which hold necessarily for human judgment. Yet, as Kant is aware, each individual is presented with a unique perspective. Sensible impressions form the basis for reflective judgments; yet the presentation of these impressions to the individual is necessarily contingent. Reflective judgment specifies purposive principles implicit in the systematicity of nature, but the content of an individual's reflective judgments is constrained by the set of sensible impressions to which he is exposed, and by the context and order of their presentation. Thus, while reflective judgment constitutes the formal condition for subjective universal judgments regarding objects in experience, in practice such subjective universality might seem unattainable.

In fact, however, subjective universal reflective judgments may be attainable in practice because an intrinsic feature of reflective judgment involves taking account of the possible judgments of others. In order to establish that this intersubjective feature characterizes teleological, as well as aesthetic judgment, I will argue for the unity of reflective judgment as a faculty.[16] In developing this argument, this section (i) examines the analytic approach which grounds the use of analogical reasoning in both aesthetic and teleological judgment; and (ii) argues for the grounding of both faculties of reflective judgment in the *sensus communis*.

A. Analytic Approach

The employment of analogical reasoning in teleological judgment appears to be grounded in insights from Kant's account of aesthetic judgment. Teleological judgment, however, extends this form of analysis to produce determinate judgments regarding empirical objects in experience, and to produce judgments with practical significance. Symbolic exhibition, a fundamental procedure of teleological judgment, is clearly conceptually related to the exhibition of a rational idea necessary to specify an archetype of taste (see CJ 232 ff.). In both cases: (i) the form of the object must be subjected to a specification or categorization prior to the reflective judgment; and (ii) reflective judgment exhibits the purposive concept implicit in the form of the object in order to represent the object's significance for human judgment.

An archetype of taste must be specified relative to a 'standard idea' of the object, which is a 'common standard' for a category of object which the imagination specifies. By preconsciously comparing images, the imagination specifies a generic image of a standard specimen of the genus[17] (CJ 234). In order to exhibit beauty, however, the form of the object must be determined by 'some underlying idea of reason' (CJ 233). The presentation of a beautiful object, therefore, must exhibit the (indeterminately purposive) idea of reason which determines its form, although 'the greatest purposiveness in the structure of that shape resides merely in the judging person's idea' (CJ 233).

In a teleological judgment, the object's form is the basis for a determination that the object is a purpose of nature; and judgment

---

[16] Teleological and aesthetic judgment are both 'contained in one ability, and resting upon one principle' (FI 244).

[17] '[T]he imagination projects, as it were, one image onto another, and from the congruence of most images of the same kind it arrives at an average which serves as the common standard for all of them' (CJ 234).

exhibits the concept of that object as a purpose of nature in order to provide the basis for a representation of the highest form of realization of that object. The teleological judgment thus exhibits the determinate purposive concept implicit in the object's form.

B. *Relation to the* Sensus Communis

While reflecting a similar analytic approach, the two forms of reflective judgment are distinct in two respects. First, the purposive concept to be exhibited is determinate for teleological judgment, but indeterminate for aesthetic judgment. Second, an account of the purposiveness of the object's form can only be specified *through* an aesthetic judgment, but must be specified in advance in order to ground and warrant a teleological judgment. As a result, only teleological exhibition grounds determinate conclusions regarding the development of empirical objects.

While an aesthetic exhibition determines a concrete representation of an ideal associated with a purposive concept, a teleological judgment exhibits the concept's determinate implications for the object's optimal development. Since teleological judgement begins with determinate concepts and produces exhibitions with determinate implications, teleological exhibition, in contrast to aesthetic judgment, provides a potential basis for practical judgments.

The fundamental similarities between the two forms of reflective judgment ground Kant's assertion that both are 'contained in one ability, and resting on the same principle' (FI 244). The distinctions between their ranges of application, however, help to explain why aesthetic judgment, alone, could not provide the basis for unifying the domains of nature and freedom. Aesthetic judgment provides the basis for a form of judgment that bridges the 'gulf' between ideas of reason and the empirical world. Aesthetic judgments, however, produce no determinate principles, and therefore have no practical significance. Teleological judgment constitutes an advance because it extends the application of this form of analogical reasoning to judgments involving determinate concepts.

The two forms of exhibition in reflective judgment therefore differ both in the specificity of their content and in their potential for practical application; both, however, are expressions of a reflective faculty which supplies a necessary condition for cognition by grounding possible judgments regarding the systematicity of nature. Each form of exhibition is both possible and necessary because judgment is confronted with objects in experience whose form manifests a significance (an implicit purposive principle) which cannot be cognized employing only concepts of the understanding.[18] Judgment must reflect on the purposiveness implicit in the forms of such objects in order to determine their status within an account of the systematicity of nature.

Where an object cannot be cognized solely through concepts of the understanding, Kant refers judgment to 'the subjective conditions for exercising [our] powers'[19] (CJ 403). The 'subjective conditions for the possibility of cognition, as such' are, for Kant, the 'proportion between the cognitive powers' (understanding and the imagination) which grounds aesthetic judgment, and which 'is *also* required for the common understanding that we may presuppose in everyone' (CJ 292–3, emphasis mine). This 'common human understanding', or *sensus communis*, is a 'broadened' form of thought in which we take account, a priori, of 'everyone else's way of presenting', in order to avoid the errors which naturally arise from a particularistic perspective[20] (CJ 293).

Kant's explicit account of the *sensus communis* stresses its function in aesthetic judgment. Yet, Kant also claims that 'we must cognize judgment's aesthetic ability, together with its teleological ability, as contained in one ability and resting on the same principle, since teleological judgments . . . belong to the reflective . . . power of judgment just as much as aesthetic ones do' (FI 244).[21]

---

[18] In aesthetic judgment, we cannot specify a determinate concept of the beautiful object, while in teleological judgment, our understanding possesses no causal concept adequate to present the reciprocal causality manifested by some objects in experience.

[19] Cognition involves the subsumption of sensory impressions under concepts of the understanding. This process, in general, is referred to as the exercise of judgment. Thus, Kant's reference is clearly to the exercise of our powers of judgment, in general.

[20] The *sensus communis* is 'a power to judge that in reflecting takes account (a priori) in our thought of everyone else's way of presenting [something], in order *as it were* to compare our own judgment with human reason, and thus escape the illusion that arises from . . . mistaking subjective and private conditions for objective ones' (CJ 293).

[21] See Ginsborg (1990): 'If a judgment of taste consists in the purely formal exercise of reflective judgment, then its legitimacy cannot be plausibly separated from that of reflective judgment in its substantive, that is, cognitive employment' (75).

If (i) aesthetic and teleological judgment are contained in one ability and rest on the same principle; (ii) the principle upon which aesthetic judgment rests is merely subjective;[22] and (iii) the subjective principle of aesthetic judgment is a power to judge that takes account (a priori) of everyone else's way of presenting the object (CJ 238–9, 294); then (iv) the (subjective) principle of teleological judgment must be a power of judgment which takes account of everyone else's way of presenting.

Kant argues that the *sensus communis* constitutes a necessary condition for cognition in cases not involving aesthetic judgment (CJ 292–3), indicating that the *sensus communis* grounds judgments that are not aesthetic. Moreover, Kant refers to taste (and therefore aesthetic judgment) as 'a *kind* of *sensus communis*' (CJ 293, first emphasis mine),[23] suggesting that the *sensus communis* is a more abstract and fundamental faculty of judgment that grounds more particularly focused faculties, such as aesthetic judgment. Therefore, it seems reasonable to argue that Kant presents aesthetic judgment as merely one member of a set of faculties grounded in the *sensus communis*.

When judgment is referred to the subjective conditions for cognition in cases in which aesthetic judgment is inapplicable (because cognition of the object requires a reference to concepts, as in the case of a purpose of nature), the *sensus communis* must ground determinations through a different faculty of reflective judgment (such as teleological judgment). The members of the set of reflective faculties grounded in the *sensus communis* are, I will argue, unified by their common grounding in the faculty of broadened thought.

Yet teleological judgment is fundamentally distinct from aesthetic judgment in one feature which might seem to render problematic Kant's claim that both faculties rest on the same principle:

---

[22] '[J]udgments of taste ... have a subjective principle, which determines them only by feeling rather than by concepts' (CJ 238).

[23] Judgments of taste 'must have a subjective principle ... Such a principle, however, could only be regarded as a *common sense* ... Only under the presupposition, therefore, that there is a common sense ... can judgments of taste be made' (CJ 238); '[T]aste *is* our ability to judge a priori the communicability of the feelings that (without mediation by a concept) are connected with a given presentation' (CJ 296, emphasis mine). 'This pleasure [the basis of aesthetic judgment] must of necessity rest on the same conditions in everyone, because they are subjective conditions for the possibility of cognition, as such, and because the proportion between these two cognitive powers that is required for taste is also required for the sound and common understanding that we may presuppose in everyone' (CJ 292–3).

teleological judgment necessarily brings the understanding into a relation with reason and concepts of reason. Aesthetic judgment, in contrast, judges 'a priori the communicability of the feelings that (without mediation by a concept) are connected with a given presentation' (CJ 296).

Kant, however, appears to separate the subjective principle of aesthetic judgment (the *sensus communis*) from the aconceptual aesthetic judgment, itself.[24] Kant does not state that the *sensus communis* is the ground solely of aesthetic judgment, but that 'taste can be called a *sensus communis* more legitimately than can sound understanding' (CJ 295). Kant's explicit discussion of the *sensus communis* (CJ 293–5) makes no reference to pleasure in the formal purposiveness of the object, or to attunement between the imagination and the understanding. Rather, Kant's discussion focuses on the notion of a form of broadened thinking which 'takes account . . . of everyone else's way of presenting [something] . . . by transferring [the individual] to the standpoint of others' (CJ 293–5). When Kant returns to the relation between the *sensus communis* and aesthetic judgment, Kant refers to the explicit discussion of the *sensus communis* as a digression.[25]

While teleological judgment, unlike aesthetic judgment, is not grounded solely in an aconceptual attunement between the imagination and the understanding, the relation between the three faculties which ground teleological judgment (imagination, understanding, reason) must (it seems) instantiate the notion of 'broadened thinking', in which one 'reflects on his own judgment from a universal standpoint (which he can determine only by transferring himself to the standpoint of others)' (CJ 295). The generation of a concept of 'what the object is [meant] to be' requires the employment of analogical thinking to produce a new concept which is independent of the empirical object and holds necessarily for human reason. The fact that this product of reflective judgment is intersubjectively valid indicates that the operation of analogical reasoning (in generating the concept) has modelled, and taken account of the possible judgments of 'everyone else'.

---

[24] It is relevant to note that the title of section 40 is 'On Taste as a *Kind* of *Sensus Communis*' (emphasis added), rather than 'On Taste as the *Sensus Communis*'. Kant appears to leave open the possibility that the *sensus communis* manifests itself in faculties independent of aesthetic judgment.

[25] 'Resuming now the thread from which I have digressed, I maintain that taste can be called a *sensus communis*' (CJ 295).

Thus, Kant appears to require that teleological judgments must be in some sense intersubjective in character. In fact, this intersubjective character appears to be a necessary feature of teleological judgment, since, I will argue, teleological judgments must exhibit both adaptability and subjective universality. Teleological judgments must be adaptable, since the judgment assesses a sensible object within its context and judges it reflectively, reasoning from the principle embodied by the observed particulars to general principles which hold necessarily for human reason. The principle embodied by such particulars is in an important degree determined by the context in which the judgment is made. For example, if everyone plays tennis at 6.00 a.m., then a maxim of playing tennis at this time will embody a different principle (playing tennis when everyone else is playing) than the same maxim will embody if no one else plays at 6.00 a.m. (Then, the maxim might be to avoid unnecessary waiting time.)

The adaptable character of reflective judgment is of fundamental significance to Kant's idea of political judgment. If political judgment is adaptive to context, then the substantive content of the political ideal, which reflective judgment determines necessarily for human reason, will nevertheless vary as fundamental elements of the empirical context vary. For example, if a society's traditions regarding property involve notions similar to the modern idea of private property, then the society's ideal political institutions will be likely to protect rights of private property resembling those protected in most western democracies. If the society's traditional notion of property is of a common asset (as in the Greek city states, for example), then the society's ideal institutions may emphasize collective, rather than individual rights (e.g. the rights of citizens, rather than those of individuals).

The ideals of a particular culture, thus, may lack objectivity from the perspective of a different culture. From within a given culture, however, Kant's argument appears to require that such ideals will be objective, but revisable (in case additional conceptual resources become available). It will not be the case, however, that every ideal grounded in a culture's tradition will be objective, even within the culture. Since the moral faculty is subjectively constitutive (CJ 453), rational beings remain capable of evaluating and rejecting traditions which are fundamentally inconsistent with the requirements of morality. Thus, while an ideal of constitutional monarchy may be objective for some cultures, an ideal incorporating inescapable slavery will be unacceptable in all cultures.

The potential implications of adaptability in political judgment can be made more concrete by considering the general implications of Kant's analysis for evaluation of form of regime. Kant argues for representative republicanism as the ideal form of regime. Yet, if the concept of republicanism were unavailable in a particular context, teleological judgment would ground the judgment that a constitutional (or constrained) monarchy was superior to an absolute monarchy, since a constitutional monarchy embodies a higher-order purposive concept.

Kant acknowledges that adaptability is a necessary feature in aesthetic judgment[26] (CJ 234). Since teleological and aesthetic judgment are 'contained in one ability', it seems reasonable to assume that they share this characteristic. Moreover, since the formal characteristics of teleological judgment appear to require adaptability, and Kant's comments indicate that aesthetic judgment exhibits this characteristic, adaptability may plausibly be ascribed to reflective judgment in general.

Yet teleological judgment holds necessarily for human judgment; we can assert the necessity of the judgment to any other rational being. If (i) teleological judgments vary depending on the set of sensible particulars grounding the judgment; and (ii) each individual may be presented with a distinct set of sensible particulars; then (iii) the judgments can only hold necessarily for all rational agents if each agent successfully anticipates the possible judgments of others and incorporates this information in his judgment. Moreover, the consideration of the possible judgments of others must be decisive when different reflective judgments grounded in the same set of particulars are plausible.

This consideration of the possible judgments of others, however, does not reduce reflective judgment to a faculty which predicts and aggregates potential judgments. In taking account of the potential judgments of others, we consider others as rational beings operating in a particular environment with interests similar

---

[26] '[I]f . . . we try to find for this average man the average head, . . . then it is this shape which underlies the standard idea of a beautiful man *in the country where this comparison is made.* That is why, given these empirical conditions, a Negro's standard idea of the beauty of the [human] figure necessarily differs from that of the white man, that of the Chinese from that of the European' (CJ 234).

and faculties identical to our own. Thus, the intersubjective aspect of reflective judgment constitutes a form of orientation which judgment determines is necessary for rational creatures within a given context.

The centrality of the notion of intersubjective, or broadened, thought in reflective judgment helps to explain the role of analogical thinking in teleological judgment. In taking account of the possible judgments of others, we cannot take account of a phenomenon existing in experience. Rather, we must construct an account of these hypothetical judgments by 'transferring [ourselves] to the standpoint of others' (CJ 295). Since we can do this only by analogy, a principled employment of inference by analogy is necessary. Kant's explicit emphasis on the intersubjective character of the *sensus communis*, in its cognitive employment, supports such a reading.[27]

Thus, a political teleological judgment would be necessary in modality and intersubjectively universal in quantity. These two qualities of political judgment would meet the necessary conditions for the determination of a political ideal. The judgment would be intersubjective, thus legitimately grounding judgments regarding issues of collective action. In addition, the judgment would be necessary for human judgment, thus meeting Kant's criterion for just legislation: 'so long as it is not self-contradictory to say that an entire people could agree to such a law . . . the law is in harmony with right' (TP 80–1). Since teleological judgments hold necessarily for human judgment, any legislation grounded in a teleological judgment is 'in harmony with right': it is not merely conceivable, but necessary, that an entire rational people could agree to such a law.

CONCLUSION

An adequately specified Kantian political theory requires an account of a faculty of political judgment that links Kant's account of systematicity to normative conclusions arising from the relations

---

[27] A man achieves a '*broadened way of thinking*' only if he 'overrides the private subjective conditions of his judgment, into which so many others are locked, as it were, and reflects on his own judgment from a *universal standpoint* (which he can determine only by transferring himself to the standpoint of others)' (CJ 295).

of objects within that system. In particular, such an account must clarify the role of the principles of natural law in influencing and constraining the content of positive legislation.

In Chapters 4 and 5, I argue that the faculty of reflective judgment grounds judgments through which the principles of natural law may constrain and influence the content of positive law. In order to specify the implications of the pure principles of natural law for objects and relations in experience, reflective judgment must determine both: (i) the moral salience of particular objects and relations in experience; and (ii) the implications of the principles of natural law for objects and relations characterized in this way. In Chapter 4, I argue that reflective judgment performs two distinct operations. The first operation specifies the moral salience of particular objects and relations in experience. In Chapter 5, I argue that a second operation of reflective judgment specifies the practical implications of pure concepts, such as the principles of natural law. In addition, reflective judgment allows us to construct an account of intersubjective judgments grounded in pure concepts, thus deepening our understanding of the concepts and their practical implications. If reflective judgments reliably specify both moral salience and the practical implications of pure concepts, then the faculty of reflective judgment provides resources sufficient to define the relation between natural and practical law and to specify the policy implications of the principles of natural law.

In addition, the account of teleological judgment in Chapters 4 and 5 suggests a modified role for a political ideal. A full specification of such an ideal is no longer necessary, since Kant claims to have provided an account of judgment which locates any par-ti-cular empirical phenomenon relative to the lawful systematicity of nature and experience. Moreover, in specifying an account of the systematicity of relations in experience, reflective judgment exhibits the fundamental moral concept of humanity. Thus, two strands of Kant's philosophy converge. Reflective political judgments: (i) hold necessarily for human judgment; and (ii) embody the determinate implications of the moral law.

6

A Kantian Model for
Social Welfare Theory

REFLECTIVE judgment, I have argued, defines the nature of the input that objects and relations in experience provide for a moral or political judgment. Moreover, teleological judgment grounds a systematic ordering of purposes in nature and specifies a methodology relating objects or relations in experience to such an ordering. In this sense, reflective judgment provides a mode of orientation for the world of experience. As such, reflective judgment constitutes a necessary tool for the interpretation of Kant's account of right and politics.

In the *Rechtslehre*, however, Kant appears to limit the nature of the contribution which pure ideas can make to political theory: pure rational ideas ground metaphysical principles embodying formal requirements binding upon relations in experience. In deriving the metaphysical principles of right from the first principle of morality, Kant identifies a fundamental requirement of right which becomes apparent when the implications of freedom for the notion of agency are explored: rightful possession of property must be at least possible. The implications of formal right for experience seem to be limited to the claim that a legitimate state must secure the necessary conditions for the rightful possession of property.

Yet the implications of this argument for relations in experience remain frustratingly indeterminate. What form of possession must be possible? What kinds of distribution of property are necessary or legitimate? And what principle should govern policies designed to secure a legitimate distribution?

A *metaphysical* account of right necessarily abstracts away from specific features of experience, focusing on the determination of rules which can be derived a priori from the mere concept of civil society.[1] In conducting his analysis at such a high level of abstraction, Kant is able to argue for principles which hold necessarily and universally. Metaphysical principles, however, constitute an uncertain grounding for substantive political determinations.

An analysis arguing directly from metaphysical principles to substantive conclusions can ground only general principles for experience, since the argument does not incorporate information relating to the contingent aspects of objects and relations in experience. It is a basic premiss of Kant's critical theory that 'the complete determination of particulars cannot be derived from our general concepts of them' (Guyer 1993: 199, see CJ 406–7). Therefore, in order to ground a practical political theory, Kant requires an interpretation of his argument for political obligations and rights which develops the concrete implications of this argument for objects and relations in experience.

Reflective judgment constitutes a resource to address this discontinuity between general concepts (or principles) and practical determinations. Since the faculty of reflective judgment grounds judgments of moral salience, this faculty exhibits the significance (moral and political) of objects and relations in experience. Moreover, as discussed in Chapter 5, arguments in the *Critique of Judgment* employ reflective judgment to exhibit political implications of pure concepts which are quite independent of what could be derived through direct argument from a pure concept, as major premiss, to a practical determination. Thus, reflective judgment supplements determinative judgments of practical reason in constituting the elements of a just social order.

Yet reflective judgments merely exhibit rational concepts. While Kant's exhibition of the rational concept of humanity defines the contours of Kant's political theory, it is too abstract to ground particular policy judgments. If the faculty of reflective judgment is to ground normative political judgments for experience, Kant must identify intermediate empirical concepts, grounded in the idea of humanity, through which we can apply the idea of humanity to empirical intuitions (see Guyer 1990: 35). Kant's deduction of the metaphysical principles of right provides such a source of intermediate concepts. As I will argue below, several central arguments in

[1] Kant defines 'metaphysical' as concerned with 'the a priori condition under which alone objects whose concept must be given empirically can be further determined a priori' (CJ 181).

'Public Right' (part II of the *Rechtslehre*) are most cogent when understood as reflective exhibitions of metaphysical principles.

The scope of Kant's analysis in the *Rechtslehre* transcends a merely metaphysical inquiry. While Kant's argument is explicitly addressed to the deduction of merely metaphysical principles of right, Kant argues for an account of justice which is to ground not merely metaphysical principles, but 'a system of laws for a people' (MJ 311). The legislators creating such a system would necessarily take into account not merely the formal nature of objects, but specific facts about objects and relations in the context of a particular state of affairs. In fact, Kant's substantive arguments in the *Rechtslehre* often: (i) require a methodology capable of mediating the discontinuity between general concepts and practical determinations; and (ii) employ the reflective methodology of symbolic representation to justify their conclusions.

Such a claim might seem puzzling, since most commentators have assumed that the *Rechtslehre* merely deduces metaphysical principles from a set of premises limited to pure ideas and formal concepts of objects. In the *Rechtslehre*, Kant in fact argues for both metaphysical first principles and practical principles governing the specific content of legislation and the nature of institutions.[2] Reflective judgment is relevant to Kant's arguments in the *Rechtslehre*, I will argue, because Kant's analytic style alters when he addresses substantive and practical, as opposed to formal and abstract, political issues. Metaphysical principles are derived merely from pure principles and formal notions of objects. But substantive arguments to particular policy conclusions, particularly in 'Public Right', employ methods of argument characteristic of reflective judgment, including symbolic representation and inference by analogy.

Thus, Kant's arguments for substantive political conclusions involve inferences from complex symbolic images. In the first five pages of 'Public Right', we encounter the general will, the social contract, the sovereign as supreme proprietor of the land, and citizens 'relinquishing' their provisional freedom in order to 'take up' rightful freedom. Efforts to assess these passages as instances of

---

[2] General principles regarding institutions include: (i) republican government as 'the only constitution that accords with right' (MJ 340); and (ii) authority of the sovereign to administer the economy (MJ 325). Specific principles governing policy include: (i) the state's authority to provide income maintenance to the poor (MJ 325–6); and (ii) the requirement of a death penalty for murder (MJ 334).

arguments from pure concepts to metaphysical principles will necessarily misconstrue Kant's methods and goals. Interpreted in light of Kant's explicit methodology for inference by analogy, however, these passages illustrate Kant's method of reflective argument from pure principles to practical political judgments.

In concluding the introduction to the *Rechtslehre*, Kant appears to suggest that arguments in the *Rechtslehre* are to be read as applications of reflective political judgment. Kant asserts that the *law* which embodies the notion of 'freedom of everyone under the principle of universal freedom' is, in fact, 'the *construction* of that concept' (MJ 232). The *Rechtslehre* is to execute such a construction, which will constitute a 'presentation of that concept' (MJ 233).

Kant's emphasis on *presentation* and *construction* echoes his employment of these notions in his account of symbolic exhibition, which constitutes an important component of the methodology of reflective judgment. Reflective judgment employs methods of construction and exhibition precisely because such methods are necessary in order to make possible judgments grounded in pure principles, but regulating contingent particulars in experience. Since the *Rechtslehre* is to provide an account of 'a system of laws for a people', reflective judgment, which makes possible substantive judgments regarding contingent particulars, appears to constitute a necessary element of Kant's account of right.

The passage cited from the *Rechtslehre* could, however, be read as merely a variant description of the *Rechtslehre*'s narrowly metaphysical project: the derivation of metaphysical principles from premises consisting merely of pure concepts and formal notions of empirical objects. In fact, Kant notes that in the analysis of right, as in the case of pure mathematical reasoning, 'reason has taken care to furnish the understanding as far as possible with a priori intuitions for the construction of the concept of right' (MJ 233). Thus, the *Rechtslehre* passage might refer to a process of reasoning limited to the consideration of pure principles and a priori intuitions of the formal properties of objects.

Such a reading would seem natural if Kant's reference to the role of a priori intuitions were taken to bar any consideration of information relating to the contingent status of objects in experience. As I have argued in Chapter 5, however, reflective judgment involves a broadened form of thought in which we take account, a priori, of 'everyone else's way of presenting' objects and relations in experience (CJ 293).

Thus, Kant's reference to a priori intuitions need not be taken to limit political analysis, in the account of right, to the relation of pure concepts to intuitions regarding the formal properties of objects. Rather, through the faculty of reflective judgment, individuals incorporate into their reasoning intuitions of 'everyone else's way of presenting' phenomena in experience. Thus, the method of symbolic exhibition constitutes a schema of the a priori workings of reflective judgment, much as the categorical imperative constitutes a schema of the moral motivation which we experience a priori.

In 'What is Orientation in Thinking?',[3] Kant suggests the relation between: (i) reason's exercise of the faculty of reflective judgment; and (ii) the reflective methodology he describes in the *Critique of Judgment*. In this essay, Kant discusses pure reason's method of self-orientation when 'it seeks to extend its sphere beyond the frontiers of experience and no longer encounters any objects of intuition whatsoever' (WOT 239–40). Since no intuitions are available for such an inquiry, reason proceeds here through the investigation of concepts. After ascertaining that the relevant concept is 'free from contradiction', reason 'reduce[s] at least the *relationship* between the object in question and objects of experience to pure concepts of the understanding'. Through this process, we 'think of something supra-sensory as capable of being applied by our reason to the world of experience' (240).

Reason's self-orientation to the super-sensible is clearly analogous to the process of inference by analogy which underlies Kant's account of symbolic exhibition. As discussed in Chapter 5, symbolic exhibition '[serves] as a means for reproducing concepts [to which no sensible intuition can be adequate] in accordance with the imagination's law of association' (CJ 352). Judgment 'applies' the concept to a sensible intuition to which we reflectively relate the concept by analogy. Analogy provides a reliable ground for such an application only when the 'basis' on which we draw our inference is 'the same' in the two objects compared (CJ 464 n.).

Such an 'identical basis' must therefore constitute a schema of the 'relationship' (between the supersensible subject of the inquiry and some sensible object) which reason reduces to a concept of the understanding. Thus, it seems reasonable to assume that Kant's discussion of symbolic exhibition itself constitutes a schema of

[3] Makkreel (1990: 154–71) and Gibbons (1994: 176–82) provide helpful discussions of this essay.

reason's process of orientation in inquiring into the implications of rational concepts when intuitive data is inadequate.

I will argue for an interpretation of Kant's doctrine of right with determinate substantive implications for a specific subject of positive legislation: social welfare. As discussed in Chapter 1, Kant's account of right might seem to present a natural basis for a welfare theory designed to rectify institutional coercion or exploitation. A legitimate state must ensure the free exercise of the innate right to freedom. Therefore, if institutional features of civil society constitute severe obstacles to such an exercise, then social intervention to redress would seem not merely permissible, but required.

Two objections to such an argument are central in the standard interpretation of Kant's theory of right. Chapters 1 and 2 examine, and reject, the claim that Kant's argument for natural law imposes severe constraints on activities of the state, barring social welfare activities. Even if such a claim does not count decisively against state welfare interventions, however, Kantian politics seems to offer no determinate basis for specifying the substance of a welfare policy. Thus, any attempt to specify a Kantian theory of social welfare must address and resolve the 'content' problem.

In this chapter, I will argue that reflective political judgment plausibly maps the relation between Kant's metaphysical principles of right and substantive welfare applications, and that reflective political judgment grounds the outline of a theory of social welfare which can be elaborated to determine the requirements of a fully developed Kantian account.

In section 1, I will examine the role of reflective judgment in grounding a reflective interpretation of the passages of the *Rechtslehre* relating to social welfare. In sections 2 and 3, I will develop the substantive implications of that interpretation.

1. FORM, SUBSTANCE, AND REFLECTIVE JUDGMENT

In this section I will argue that the faculty of reflective political judgment provides a basis for resolving a specific question in Kant's account of right: how is the relation between natural and positive law to be specified in order to give content to the notion of the 'rightful condition' of civil society? Moreover, since Kant defines 'rightful condition' in terms of justice in the distribution of goods, an account of the substantive implications of this notion will also develop important aspects of Kant's political theory directly relevant to a Kantian account of social welfare.

A. Natural and Positive Law

In Chapter 1, I argued that the *Rechtslehre* underdetermines the extension of the principles of natural law. Legislation, and positive law generally, must embody the principles of natural law derived in 'Private Right' (see p. 13 above; Gregor 1991: 16). Yet Kant offers no clear account of the relation between positive and natural law.

This relation is of great importance for two reasons. First, Kant asserts that a rightful civil condition can exist only 'in conformity with the conditions of freedom and equality' (MJ 315). We therefore require some specification of the substantive constraints and requirements which these conditions impose upon policy. The principles of natural law embody the necessary legislative and institutional conditions for a society grounded in: (i) the realization of each citizen's innate right to freedom; and (ii) the recognition of each citizen as equal in their claim to the realization of such an innate right. Yet in order to generate a body of law which is in conformity with these fundamental commitments, the legislature requires a clear account of the relation between natural law and positive civil law.

Second, if natural law specifies certain necessary conditions for a rightful civil condition, these conditions must be met before such a rightful condition can exist. For example, Kant argues that 'right' requires the 'universal reciprocal coercion' of all (MJ 232). Therefore, all coercive laws must apply universally. But suppose a legislature enacted only decrees, and that all coercive measures were authorized on a case-by-case basis. Such a legislature could enact decrees which effectively protected the property of all, while at the same time failing to enact a body of legislation which realized universal reciprocal coercion. Such a body of legislation would fail to satisfy the threshold requirement for a rightful condition.

While this example relies upon a substantive requirement which is explicit in Kant's metaphysical argument, other necessary conditions are implicit but unspecified. For example, the sovereign, as supreme proprietor, must specify a rightful 'apportionment' of the property among members of civil society; yet Kant does not specify a distributive principle to ground such a distribution. If a society fails to distribute property in accordance with the requirements of natural law, the distribution may fail to be 'in accordance with the conditions of freedom and equality', in which case, a rightful condition will not exist. Thus, unless the requirements of natural law can be concretely specified, legislatures will be unable to determine whether they have satisfied even the minimum criteria for a just social condition.

Reflective political judgments exhibit the practical significance of formal notions, making explicit requirements that such notions may impose upon relations in experience. The principles of natural law identified in Kant's metaphysical analysis are formal principles which require just such an exhibition of their significance for relations in a civil condition. In this section, I will examine the work which reflective judgment can do in specifying the practical significance of the principles of natural law in Kant's account of public right, particularly as that account bears upon Kant's comments on social welfare.

B. Natural Law and Public Right

Kant's account of natural law grounds two fundamental metaphysical principles. First, civil society must guarantee the possibility of rightful possession of property (Juridical Postulate). Second, such a guarantee can only be effective if all members of society are united in a civil condition under the coercive power of a joint general will (Postulate of Public Law).

Rightful possession of property is defined by the legislation of the general will, and therefore can only exist as constituted within a civil condition. Thus, the principles grounding the civil condition define the nature of the distribution to be protected in civil society. The general will determines what claims to property can be rightful; therefore, no such claims can be rightful unless grounded in the principles defining social right. Thus, the sovereign, or general will, must specify the distributive principle which is to structure such a distribution.

While the analysis of natural law fails to define the nature of a just distribution of property, 'Public Right' explores the possible ground for such a distribution by developing an argument first explored in the *Critique of Judgment*. In this argument, Kant asserts that the idea of 'the transformation of a large people into a state' may be 'elucidated' through an analogy to a self-organized being (CJ 375 n.). This analogy illuminates the relation of the members of the state to the whole: 'while each member contributes to making the whole possible, the idea of that whole should in turn determine the member's position and function' (CJ 375 n.).

The analogy highlights the importance of the idea of the whole in structuring the social position occupied by the individual: socially determinative concepts such as rights are defined only in the context of realizing the idea of a social whole (a rightful civil condition). In particular, the idea of a rightful civil condition, in Kant's account, requires that definitive right-claims can be constituted only after individuals have united to enter civil society.

Since *all* right-claims originating in the state of nature are thus merely provisional, it is central to Kant's argument that civil society must exist *before* definitive property rights can be established. Each individual in civil society has 'relinquished entirely' his provisional rights in order to take up the rights apportioned to him within civil society. Property rights within civil society are 'apportioned' to each subject by the sovereign (representing the united general will) (MJ 316). Thus, individuals surrender their provisional claims from the state of nature in order to 'take . . . up again' rights backed by the coercive sanctions of the sovereign (MJ 315).

The necessary transformation of merely contingent claims to property into claims of right is 'represented' by a second analogy, that of the sovereign as supreme proprietor apportioning society's collectively held property.[4] The sovereign, as 'proprietor of the land', must 'apportion' (MJ 316) property in accordance with a principle of *division* (*Einteilung*), rather than with principles of *aggregation* (*Aggregation*) (MJ 324). The analogy of the sovereign as proprietor thus embodies the notion of social transformation.

Moreover, such a transformation necessarily involves the transfer of property to the jurisdiction of the sovereign. In order to

---

[4] 'This supreme proprietorship is . . . only an Idea of civil union that serves to represent in accordance with concepts of right the necessary union of everyone within the people under a general public possessor, so that the determination of the particular property of each is in accordance with the necessary formal principle of *division* . . . instead of with principles of *aggregation* (which proceeds empirically from the parts to the whole' (MJ 323–4).

realize the idea of 'the necessary union of the property of everyone within the people under a common public possessor' (MJ 323), the sovereign requires the power to tax private property, and to apply the proceeds to the costs of administering public affairs (see MJ 325). Kant's arguments do not suggest merely that the sovereign must retain and apply property in order to secure the continued existence of civil society. Rather, Kant asserts that the sovereign must realize the idea of 'necessary union of . . . property . . . under a common public possessor' which represents Kant's ideal of distributive justice.[5]

The notion that the sovereign may tax private property in order to realize an ideal of justice in the distribution of property might appear to violate Kant's requirement that all state exercises of coercive power must be justified as necessary in order to '[hinder] a hindrance to freedom' (MJ 231). In taxing private property to finance the realization of public goods, the sovereign might appear to coerce without such a justification.

Such a criticism, however, can be sustained only if individuals possess privileged claims to property independent of, and prior to, the norms of the civil condition. As we have seen, however, Kant argues that rightful claims to property exist only *within* a civil condition, and derive their legitimacy from the constitution of a united general will. Moreover, Kant argues that property may be possessed 'in common' by 'all those (joined together) who forbid or suspend one another's use of it' (MJ 250). Thus, an underlying distributive principle which apportions some specified percentage of citizens' earnings to funds 'possessed in common', and devoted to the realization of a rationally required social goal, appears perfectly consistent with Kant's reservations regarding the use of coercive power by the state.

Finally, a rightful condition will only be established if the sovereign apportions property in accordance with a *just* principle of distribution.[6] Since social transformation is a necessary condition of

---

[5] The 'union of the property of everyone under a common public possessor', in fact, represents the requirement of right that 'the determination of the particular property of each' is to be 'in accordance with the necessary formal principle of *division* . . . instead of with principles of *aggregation*' (MJ 323–4).

[6] '[I]t is only in conformity with the conditions of freedom and equality that this people can become a state and enter into a civil constitution' (MJ 315).

rightful social life, Kant's account of right requires a principle capable of grounding the transformation of property holdings.[7]

The required principle is to constitute the origin and foundation of all rightful claims to property; therefore, the principle cannot be grounded in appeals to any existing norms or practices governing the distribution of property. Since the required principle cannot be grounded in practice, it must be derived from the mere concept of human beings as holders of property rights in a condition of public right. Since (i) the notion of public right merely requires mutual external freedom; and (ii) the relation of humans to property rights remains to be defined; therefore (iii) the distributive criterion must be grounded in some quality necessarily associated with the mere concept of a human being. Only one salient quality characterizes human beings generally: humanity (defined as '[t]he capacity to set oneself an end')[8] (DV 392). While Kant's notion of humanity constitutes a moral, rather than a political, concept, this notion grounds the innate right to freedom. All members of the civil condition are equally possessors of this right, and civil society is legitimate precisely to the extent that it secures protection for this right. Therefore, Kant's account identifies all members of society as equal in their possession of the fundamental quality which defines the political status of members of a rightful civil condition.

The equal status of all citizens, as possessors of the innate right to freedom, is represented by a final analogy: the idea of a general will in which all citizens participate equally as joint authors.[9] This status (equal authorship of the general will) represents both (i) the

[7] An inquiry designed to identify a criterion of legitimacy for legislation does not violate the spirit of Kant's assertion that subjects 'ought not to rationalize' concerning the origin of the state's authority (MJ 318). The inquiry is intended to specify the necessary conditions of a rightful condition. Thus, the inquiry is designed, not to undermine any existing regime, but to direct the progress of social institutions.

[8] 'The capacity to set oneself an end—any end whatsoever—is what characterizes humanity' (DV 392). While it could be argued that merit constitutes an additional quality which can and should be considered in determining the allocation of property, in fact no fundamental Kantian principle or argument defines how merit could be considered as a factor in such a distribution, or what counts as merit for this purpose. Rather, Kant's political theory is to constitute the terms in which social merit is to be calculated.

[9] '[O]nly the concurring and united will of all . . . and so only the general united will of the people, can be legislative' (MJ 314). '[A] public law which defines for everyone that which is permitted and prohibited by right . . . requires no less than the will of the entire people' (TP 77).

equality among members of civil society; and (ii) an interpretation of that equality. First, each member possesses an equal claim upon the protection of the state as an equal possessor of the innate right to freedom. Second, each member of society has the same purpose (realization of his innate right to freedom) in entering civil society. Thus, innate freedom constitutes both: (i) the ground for the constitution of the general will, and thus of civil society; and (ii) the irreducibly basic content of the general will.

The notion of equality implicit in the equal status of individuals as authors of the general will is best understood in terms of Kant's analogy comparing 'the transformation of a large body of people into a state' to a self-organized being (CJ 375 n.). In this analogy, individual members of civil society are represented as parts which are reciprocally cause and effect of the idea of the whole.

I have argued that Kant employs inference by analogy in reflective judgment to: (i) ground judgments specifying a purposive concept implicit in the form of the object or relation; and (ii) derive an ideal notion of the object or relation from reflection upon the specified concept. In this case, Kant's analogy exhibits the reciprocal causality implicit in the relation of individual members to the collective civil condition.

Kant's representation of members of civil society as joint co-authors of the general will establishes the legislative faculties of each member as a structural element of the reciprocal causal relation between civil society and its members. Moreover, since the general will constitutes the ends of civil society, Kant's representation establishes the ability to form and pursue ends ('humanity') of each member as a structural element of this reciprocal causal relation.

In order to derive an ideal notion of the object within the framework of Kantian political judgment, the exhibited purposive concept must be considered in the context of Kant's hierarchy of purposive concepts, ranked according to the degree of unconditioned causality manifested. The relation between individual members and the idea of a civil condition will increasingly approach the unconditioned as individuals become increasingly adept at forming and pursuing ends independent of any empirical interest.

In an *unconditioned* realization of the idea of civil society, therefore, all members would realize to the maximum degree their faculty of humanity (defined as man's 'aptitude for setting himself purposes' (CJ 431).[10] In a fully realized rightful condition, all members of the civil condition will be assured an equal *opportunity* to realize their capacity to form and pursue ends.

To summarize, Kant argues from two analogies which exhibit: (i) the notion of society as a self-organized entity characterized by reciprocal causality; and (ii) the notion of social transformation implicit in the argument for the postulate of practical reason. These analogies jointly define a rightful condition as a state in which members are assured equal access to the opportunity to realize an unconditioned form of purposiveness (humanity), and thus the capacity to define institutions and rules constitutive of an ideal civil society. A just distributive principle will therefore respect the equal humanity of each member by assuring equal access to the opportunity to realize her purposive capacities.

Equal access to opportunity does not, however, imply the right to equality of outcome. Kant argues explicitly that right is consistent with 'the utmost inequality of the mass in the degree of its possessions' (TP 75). Rather, equality as a member of the general will implies that society must respect and protect the individual's 'aptitude in general for setting himself purposes' (CJ 431).

Nevertheless, the realization of a rightful condition requires the actualization of a form of life which embodies the commitment to humanity as a substantive concept, not merely the avoidance of unjust forms of social organization. While a society may in fact fail to realize this ideal, a society which aims to achieve a rightful condition must adopt a commitment to humanity as the goal grounding its institutions and social legislation. The commitment must be not merely to avoid legislation or institutions inconsistent with this goal, but to work positively to ensure that empirical conditions, in particular the operations of political and economic institutions and the distribution of property, do not prevent its realization. Therefore, while a rightful condition will not necessarily eliminate inequality, the sovereign must avoid a distribution of property which cedes to the advantaged the power to coerce the disadvantaged and hinders the realization (by the disadvantaged) of unconditioned humanity. A state which protects formal property rights, but whose

---

[10] Not coincidentally, the duty to respect the humanity of all other rational beings grounds the innate right to freedom, and thus the necessity of forming a just civil condition. The purpose of the civil condition is to provide a context in which all may realize the faculty of humanity.

ordinary operations routinely permit a privileged class to coerce other members of society through the exercise of economic or other power, has failed to realize a rightful condition.

It could be objected that Kant's inferences by analogy, in general, perform a cognitive rather than normative function, merely providing reassurance that humanity is in fact progressing. This claim, however, describes only a subset of Kant's applications of analogical reasoning. In fact, Kant's employment of analogical reasoning in his political works exhibits the content of moral concepts which are themselves normative for rational beings. Just as the final purpose of nature constitutes an obligation because it renders intelligible the normative implications of a moral concept, the analogies of the general will, the supreme proprietor and the apportionment of rights all exhibit notions whose normativity derives from their direct grounding in the fundamental Kantian moral concept of humanity. As the derivation of the final purpose of nature exhibits the implications of the notion of humanity, the analogies characteristic of Kant's political thought ground exhibitions of subsidiary moral and political notions *derived from* the notion of humanity.

Thus, as argued in Chapter 5, the task of sustaining the unconditioned quality of man's purposiveness and the task of respecting man's humanity coincide. Our obligation to respect humanity in human institutions coincides with our reflective judgment that just institutions must sustain and support man's purposive capacities.

While the obligation to realize a society embodying a commitment to humanity might seem to constitute merely a wide and underdetermined duty, this duty is sufficiently well specified to impose certain determinate requirements on forms of social organization. In particular, a rightful condition must avoid inherently coercive conditions, in which, through lack of access: (i) disadvantaged individuals may be 'bound by others to more than [the disadvantaged] can in turn bind them' (MJ 237); and (ii) the disadvantaged lack any reasonable hope of 'work[ing] . . . up from this passive condition' (MJ 315). Under such circumstances, the disadvantaged are consigned to a condition in which the realization of their capacity for purposive agency is sacrificed for the benefit of the advantaged individuals. The disadvantaged are treated 'merely as a means', and their right to freedom is violated in the most profound fashion. Thus, a just distributive principle must, at a minimum, be designed to prevent the development of inherently coercive social conditions.

If the commitment to the equal status of citizens as human (possessing the potential capacity for unconditioned purposive agency) is to affect the substantive content of a just distributive principle, the notion of equal status must be translated into terms relevant to the content of a distributive principle. As noted, equal status does not necessarily ground a claim to equal resources or equal utility. What, in fact, does a commitment to the equal status of citizens, as possessors of a potentially unconditioned 'aptitude' for forming and pursuing purposes, require of a social distribution? At a minimum, agents must have equal access to the opportunity to develop their capacity for purposes; but what substantive requirement is implicit?

Kant argues that the capacity to set ends is realized through cultivation of the 'crude predispositions of [human] nature' through practice and 'culture in general' (DV 392). In order to cultivate the 'highest' of these predispositions, 'the faculty of concepts', man must 'diminish his ignorance by instruction' (DV 387). In addition, man realizes his capacity to set ends by cultivating his natural powers, including the powers of the body, imagination, taste, and logic[11] (DV 444–5). In cultivating these powers, in particular the faculty of concepts, man 'raise[s] himself from the crude state of his nature' and approaches the unconditioned (by empirical incentives) exercise of his capacity to set himself ends (DV 387).

Thus, it is possible, within the framework of a Kantian analysis, to identify elements necessary for the realization of purposive agency. Individuals will be unable to develop their aptitude for forming and pursuing their own projects if they lack access to adequate means and opportunities to exercise their faculty for purposes and to develop their natural powers. Necessary elements for the realization of purposive agency would therefore include: (i) resources; (ii) education; (iii) political and economic power; (iv) the social bases of self-respect; and (v) social networks of opportunity and status. The realization of a rightful civil condition appears

---

[11] 'Man has a duty to himself to cultivate his natural powers . . . as a means to all sorts of ends. Man owes it to himself . . . not to leave idle and, as it were, rusting away the natural predispositions and capacities that his reason can someday use' (DV 444).

to require compensatory interventions to remedy unequal access to such necessary elements.

Yet Kant argues that morally practical law, including legislation governing external relations,[12] must be 'universal legislation' (CPr 41) that is 'valid in the same form for all rational beings' (CPr 21). How are laws that are valid in the *same form* for all rational beings to regulate the implementation of policies requiring differentiated compensatory interventions (policies requiring that, for example, a *particular* individual is entitled to a *specific* form of intervention to address his or her (perhaps) *unique* form of disadvantage)?[13]

Provisions of positive law state universal rules regulating relations in experience. In order to regulate relations in experience, however, such legislation will in many cases require a set of subordinate laws or administrative rules to define the specific bearing of the universal rule on particular relations falling within the rule's jurisdiction. Thus, 'a metaphysics of morals cannot dispense with principles of application . . . in order to *show* [in experience] what can be inferred from universal moral principles' (MJ 216–17). Such subordinate laws or rules will be necessary in order to implement substantive requirements of right (such as the requirement that all subjects receive equal access to opportunity), but also in order to regulate the application of legal concepts such as contract. Any viable system of contract law will require a system of rules specifying, for example, remedies to apply in case of various forms of incomplete or nonconforming performance.

In order to implement a substantive requirement of law, subordinate rules must designate the means best designed to realize the substantive requirement. The explicit language of the law will, to some extent, limit the set of relevant means or policies. Thus, only policies that affect the distribution of goods will be appropriate to implement a law requiring equal access to resources. The choice of a best policy option, however, will require a judgment that a particular policy is, in fact, best designed to realize the purpose(s) of the legislation. Since the principle of natural law that grounds a provision of positive legislation constitutes the definitive statement of the purpose that the legislation is to realize, the policy best

---

[12] Moral law includes both juridical law, which is 'directed merely to external actions and their conformity to law', and ethical laws, which 'require that they (the laws) themselves be the determining grounds of actions' (MJ 214).

[13] I am grateful to Richard Tuck for urging me to provide an explicit response to this objection.

designed to implement a provision of law will be designed to realize the purpose manifest in the underlying natural law. The principles of natural law thus narrow the range of appropriate policy choices and determine what considerations are relevant in justifying the choice of a particular policy.

Suppose, for example, that positive legislation, designed to embody the principle of natural law requiring that a rightful condition be in accordance with conditions of freedom and equality, requires the provision to all members of society of guaranteed levels of access to certain resources (e.g. education, adequate health care, housing). Policies designed to implement the law will take the form: if case X fails to meet in manner Y the required standard of access, relief Z is necessary.[14] The provisions of this form that are most closely in conformity with the requirements of natural law will be those in which: (i) *manner Y* constitutes a threat to the agent's equal access to the ability to form and pursue ends; and (ii) *relief Z* is well constituted to address this threat.

Equal access to opportunity, as a basic principle, implies a commitment to allow individuals to determine outcomes for themselves through their choices. The choices made by individual agents determine the actual distribution of resources. This approach contrasts sharply with that of welfare egalitarians, who focus on equalizing subjective utility levels, irrespective of the choices made by individuals. By de-emphasizing the element of choice, welfare egalitarian thought remains vulnerable to paradoxes arising from self-regarding choices by individuals, such as the problems of expensive tastes[15] and ambition insensitivity.[16]

In order to develop the implications of Kant's notion of distributive justice, we require some account of the currency in which a just distribution of rights and property can be defined—a 'currency of egalitarian justice'.[17] In the following sections, I will argue for a

[14] Such legislation, while crafted to apply to a particular set of cases, nevertheless holds universally within the terms of its restrictive language. That is, any person who falls below the stated standard of access to a particular resource is entitled to a specific form of relief.

[15] Cultivating expensive tastes may improve the individual's claim to a larger share in the final distribution (see Cohen 1989).

[16] An individual's choice of a non-productive lifestyle may generate a social obligation to support the individual (see Dworkin 1981*a*, 1981*b*, Cohen 1989, Van Parijs 1990).

[17] While I have borrowed this term from Cohen (1989) to characterize the nature of the currency required, my account of the proper form for such a currency diverges sharply from his, since I argue for a capabilities distribuendum.

Kantian account of such a currency. Since this topic is touched upon, rather than developed, in the Kantian texts, I will argue from the implications of the fundamental commitments I have argued for in Kant's political thought, rather than from specific textual sources.

2. THE CURRENCY OF DISTRIBUTIVE EQUALITY

I have argued that Kant's account of the rightful condition of civil society requires that: (i) right claims are structured according to a distributive principle defined by the general will which grounds the organization of civil society; (ii) such a distributive principle must embody the equal status of members of society; and (iii) the operative notion of equality is equal possession of the potential to realize unconditioned purposiveness.

An examination of the proper composition of an egalitarian currency is structured by the heterogeneity of the goods to be distributed and the ambiguity of the term 'distribution'. I will define 'allocation' as a *process* of distributing goods among individuals, while 'distribution' will refer to a *state* which can be described by specifying the quantities of goods possessed by individuals (Elster 1992: 186).

In apportioning rights and property, the Kantian sovereign will proceed on a principle of guaranteeing to each citizen equal access to the opportunity to realize her purposive agency. Potential to realize purposive agency will be affected by the distribution of three distinct kinds of goods: (i) allocable goods: goods which can be allocated directly (e.g. money); (ii) non-allocable goods: goods whose distribution may be affected by the allocation of other goods (e.g. welfare, self-respect, health); (iii) natural endowments: goods whose distribution cannot be affected by allocation (e.g. endogenous talents).

The sovereign can directly control the distribution of only the first category of goods. Moreover, direct manipulation of the distribution of allocable goods will in many cases fail to produce proportionate alterations in the distribution of non-allocable goods, such as welfare or the capacity for purposive agency, since individuals convert goods to welfare improvements with differing degrees of efficiency.

I will argue that the distribution of non-allocable goods is the proper focus for a Kantian distributive principle. The fundamental goal of Kantian distributive justice is to equalize access to the opportunity to develop one's capacity for unconditioned purposiveness, a non-allocable good. Therefore, allocable goods are valued, not unconditionally, but because, and to the extent, they are instrumental to the realization of the aptitude to act purposively. While the reallocation of allocable goods may be a necessary condition of equal access to the aptitude to act purposively, the reallocation of allocable goods remains a precondition, not the substantive goal, of a Kantian distributive principle.

In addition, the distribution of natural endowments structures the distribution problem, since asymmetries in ability to translate allocable into non-allocable goods[18] appear to result directly from asymmetries in endowments. The manner in which allocable goods must be apportioned to realize any particular distribution of non-allocable goods is determined by the ability of individuals to convert goods into non-allocable goods, which, in turn, is determined by the distribution of natural endowments.

A Kantian distributive principle, therefore, will require a reallocation of allocable goods to achieve a principled distribution of non-allocable goods. Moreover, even within Kantian theory, absolutely equal access to opportunity may be unattainable or unattractive. Rather, the distributive principle must identify the category of non-allocable goods to be redistributed and define the principles which structure a justifiable distribution.

Thus, a Kantian distributive principle must first designate the non-allocable good(s) which will be the ultimate distribuendum. Second, such a principle must define what would constitute a justifiable distribution of that category of goods (e.g. the *kind* of relation that is to be structured between the distributions of allocable and non-allocable goods).

Designating the Distribuendum Good

At the highest level of generality, non-allocable goods may be organized, according to the nature of their effect on the recipient, into three categories: (i) welfare; (ii) resources; and (iii)

[18] This asymmetry applies to, but is not limited to, asymmetries in converting allocable goods into welfare. Agents also experience asymmetries converting allocable goods into capacities.

capabilities. *Welfare* is defined as the utility derived from allocations of allocable goods. *Resources* are the stock of goods available to the agent to facilitate her pursuit of her ends. *Capabilities* are the actual ability to perform certain functionings which the agent desires to perform. It is important to note that capabilities provide agents with the option to pursue a certain end, rather than a guarantee of success.

A capabilities distribuendum appears to offer the best currency for Kantian distributive justice, since such a distribuendum grounds the principle of distribution in the substantive basis for claims to equal political standing: equality of purposive agency. Recent work by Sen (1980, 1985) argues for capabilities equality as an account of the fundamental concerns of egalitarian thought. My sketch of a capabilities distribuendum, however, differs substantially from Sen's, since a Kantian distributive principle must assign agency freedom absolute priority over well-being freedom.

An advantage of such a capabilities distribuendum is that it avoids problems which arise if welfare or resources are chosen as the distribuendum. Welfarist compensation strategies aim to equalize welfare by compensating agents for arbitrary inequalities. Yet compensation cannot equalize welfare between individuals with radically asymmetric endowments. For example, no level of compensation can guarantee to compensate for welfare losses due to severe physical handicaps (see Cohen 1989, Kymlicka 1990).

Resourcist distributive strategies aim to equalize access to essential resources (see Dworkin 1981*a*, 1981*b*). Yet equal allocation of essential resources does not necessarily realize equal capacity to realize ends, since different individuals will vary in their capacity to transform resources into capacities to pursue ends.

A capabilities approach does not attempt to equalize outcomes. Rather, this approach attempts to ensure that the inevitable asymmetries among outcomes (relating to the realization of the capacity to realize ends) are the result of genuine choices, and not of contingencies of natural endowment or environmental influence.

This concern is particularly important for a principle which is to define the terms in which rights claims are defined and assessed, because inequalities tend to be cumulative over time. An individual's choice to develop artistic, rather than commercial, talents will limit the economic resources, and thus the opportunity to realize the capacity to form and pursue ends, of his descendants. In each succeeding generation, the limited wealth inherited will further constrain access to equal opportunity.

A just distributive principle must guarantee that such cumulative inequalities, not resulting from choices by the individual: (i) do not *result* directly from the proper operations of the principle; and (ii) are counterbalanced so that individuals are not denied equal opportunity to pursue their distinctive ends. The distributive principle must redress, rather than reinforce, such arbitrary inequalities in access to opportunity experienced by individuals choosing to pursue different forms of purposive activity. Therefore, access to the capability to pursue ends must be assured independent of morally irrelevant factors, such as: (i) arbitrary inequality in the rewards assigned to certain choices of ends; or (ii) endowments.

A capabilities distribuendum is unlike a welfare or resources distribuendum, since a policy of equalizing the distribution of capabilities does not require that the distribution of some set of goods must be equalized. Rather, all members of society are to be guaranteed access to the opportunity to realize certain fundamental capabilities which will ensure that all possess an equal opportunity to define and pursue autonomous ends. In this way, the capabilities approach attempts to minimize the impact of endowments and environment on outcomes.

An operational capabilities approach must, therefore, identify a set of relations between allocable and non-allocable goods that structures access to the ability to realize ends in different fields of endeavour. The relation will vary with the substantive area.

The significance of various non-allocable goods, and therefore the nature of a just principle of distribution, will vary over categories of purposive activity. It seems unlikely that a set of basic non-allocable goods can be specified. Rather, a set of meta-rules is necessary to govern the way in which allocable goods are to be distributed in order to facilitate the realization of capacities instrumental to the realization of ends. Moreover, the application of these rules will be determined by specific environmental and contextual factors. At a minimum, such rules must operate so that the distribution of non-allocable goods is structured to ensure that: (i) disadvantaged individuals may not be 'bound by others to more than [the disadvantaged] can in turn bind them' (MJ 237); and (ii) the disadvantaged possess a reasonable hope of 'work[ing] . . . up from this passive condition' (MJ 315).

The range of the analysis is, however, limited by the social and political focus: basic capabilities must be skills or capacities, access to which is necessary to fulfil the commitment to equal opportunity implicit in the metaphysical principles of natural law. Human beings possess rightful claims to exercise purposive agency, not to the realization of specific outcomes. Therefore, while all should be guaranteed the basic capabilities necessary to pursue their ends, none can be *guaranteed* the access to specialized capacities necessary to achieve subjective ends.

3. POLICY IMPLICATIONS: ALLOCATION OF WELFARE RESOURCES

In order to identify policy implications of a capabilities-based distributive principle, I will examine the implications of such a principle for antipoverty policy in the United States. I will examine two questions: (i) should antipoverty policy give priority to income supplementation or compensatory intervention; and (ii) should income supplementation be provided entirely in cash or partially in kind?

A. *Income Supplementation or Compensatory Intervention*

The federal government and the states provide two basic forms of redistributive antipoverty policy: (i) income supplementation, which may be provided in cash or in kind; and (ii) compensatory intervention.[19] Only the second form of intervention is intended to develop the capabilities of programme participants. Therefore, if capabilities constitute the fundamental value to be promoted by welfare interventions, it might seem that compensatory intervention should be categorically favoured over income supplementation.

Survey data, however, suggests that the major compensatory initiatives designed to increase the skills of the disadvantaged failed to enhance the capabilities of their participants. Studies of the

---

[19] Compensatory interventions include education, training, and subsidized employment.

effectiveness of the CETA programme, in the late 1970s, and Work Incentive Demonstration Projects, in the mid-1980s, identified the same result: manpower interventions produced increases in earnings which were statistically significant, but not large[20] (see Bassie and Ashenfelter 1986, Goldman et al. 1986, Barnow 1987). The earning increases identified seem to result from credentialling effects rather than from skill acquisition.

In addition, income supplementation and compensatory intervention serve the needs of different members of the low-income population. Income assistance defines the living conditions for those least able to support themselves: children, the disabled, mothers of pre-school children. The level of income support provided, therefore, has a direct effect on the quality of life experienced by those receiving such support.

Compensatory interventions serve the needs of the employable poor: adults who are not disabled or encumbered with young children.[21] Unemployment for many, although far from all, members of this group is cyclical or frictional. In addition, as noted above, the effectiveness of training programmes to improve employability has been challenged.

Income supplementation competes directly, for funds, with compensatory interventions. Since (i) income supplementation is required to satisfy the urgent and basic needs of persons dependent upon state assistance; and (ii) the effectiveness of manpower interventions has been questioned; (iii) policy-makers have found it logical to give income assistance some degree of priority over investments in manpower policy.

Yet income support merely sustains recipients in a dependent and unproductive existence. Not only do the dependent lead unproductive and humiliating existences; in addition, their support is constantly endangered by the rapidly shifting moods of the electorate.

Moreover, programme studies may have understated the impact of compensatory interventions. First, the programmes studied were

---

[20] CETA participants experienced a $200–600 increase in annual earnings. Work Incentive Demonstration participants experienced increases in annual earnings of approximately $700.

[21] Compensatory education in pre-school and elementary and secondary education constitute special cases, since the interventions are not restricted to individuals who are unemployed or dependent on state subsidies.

short-term and low-budget.[22] Second, the methodology employed in analysing programme results may systematically understate the impacts of manpower programmes (see Erlebacher 1970). Finally, unobserved heterogeneity among programme participants may obscure impacts experienced by subgroups.[23]

The argument for compensatory intervention, therefore, remains compelling. The problem for antipoverty policy is to define a principled basis for trade-offs between income assistance and compensatory interventions.

In the preceding section, I suggested that a general distributive principle structuring relations in a political society must focus on the distribution of non-allocable goods. In the context of antipoverty policy, capabilities constitute the non-allocable goods whose distribution is to be structured. The distribution of non-allocable goods, however, can only be affected through redistribution of allocable goods.

Two categories of allocable goods can be reallocated to affect the distribution of capabilities: (i) necessary resources, and (ii) education/training. Access to necessary resources, such as food, shelter, and medical care, constitutes a *precondition* to the realization of capabilities. A training programme can only be effective if its participants are minimally well nourished and in reasonably good health. Income and in-kind support provide access to such necessary resources.

An antipoverty policy which provided no more than access to necessary resources, however, would not provide the disadvan-

---

[22] Taggart (1981) discusses factors which may have led to poor programme performance: (i) programmes experienced violent fluctuations in funding levels, service mix, and organizational structure; (ii) resources for programmes designed to address structural unemployment were allocated according to relative unemployment rates, preventing coherent long-term planning; (iii) fluctuations in funding led to programmes of minimal complexity and duration, designed for rapid expansion and contraction rather than optimal service delivery; (iv) programmes were unable to staff with high-quality personnel because of uncertain funding and lack of programme continuity.

[23] Consider the following hypothetical example: (i) 40 per cent of participants are 'job-ready'; 30 per cent are moderately disadvantaged; and 30 per cent are severely disadvantaged; (ii) the 'job-ready' experience a negative impact of $1,500 on earnings; (iii) the moderately disadvantaged experience no change; and (iv) the severely disadvantaged experience a positive impact of $3,500 on earnings. The programme impact observed on an undifferentiated population would be $(0.4) * (-\$1500) + (0.3) * (0) + (0.3) * (+\$3500) = +\$450$. The sizeable impact on the severely disadvantaged would be concealed within the aggregate information.

taged with greater access to capabilities. Interventions providing access to the skills necessary for autonomous self-sufficiency are required to begin to restructure the distribution of capabilities.

Income support, as a precondition of an effective antipoverty policy, is essential while individuals lack the resources or capabilities to provide for themselves. As the disadvantaged obtain greater access to resources, however, the marginal value of income supplementation declines relative to compensatory interventions.

Based on the foregoing discussion, the following three propositions suggest a possible framework for balancing the claims of income support and manpower policy. First, income support is necessary when it constitutes the sole source of essential resources. Second, income support provides *only* a precondition for the acquisition of capabilities, not a solution to the problem of poverty. Finally, above some threshold level of income support, funds spent on income support have diminishing marginal utility relative to funds spent on compensatory initiatives.

These propositions have two important implications for policy. First, economists have classically argued that income supplementation is the most efficient antipoverty policy. Yet if my argument is correct, a purely income-directed approach may fail to address the basic distributional problem of poverty: unequal access to capabilities. Second, a society in which inequalities can be justified to all affected individuals must provide serious compensatory interventions designed to equalize access to capabilities. Only in a society in which all share equal access to capabilities will distributive differences derive directly from the choices of the affected individuals.[24]

B. In Cash or In Kind

Assistance provided 'in kind' involves the delivery of goods or services, rather than the income necessary to obtain such services. The principal forms of assistance provided in kind include food

---

[24] Compensatory manpower interventions are generally designed to redress the absence of some skill or set of skills. Policies which seek to improve the distribution of practical capabilities, such as skills, do not address the need to equalize access to intellectual capabilities, so that the choices individuals make can be to the greatest degree possible autonomous, and free from contingent environmental influences. Compensatory education programmes may begin to address the problem of access to intellectual capabilities.

subsidies (e.g. Food Stamps), health care (e.g. Medicare and Medicaid), housing subsidies, and day care.

The goods and services provided in kind are preconditions to the attainment of capacities: individuals need to be moderately healthy and well nourished before they are able to pursue skill acquisition.

Yet providing assistance in kind, rather than in cash, may be inconsistent with the goal of assisting individuals to realize their humanity. If the individual is to realize this aptitude for setting himself purposes, he must acquire the capacity to make rational choices for himself. In-kind assistance designates a goal (e.g. elimination of hunger) independent of the choices or preferences of the aid recipients, and supplies goods or services (e.g. food or vouchers for food) designed to achieve the stipulated goal. In-kind assistance might, in fact, reinforce the learned helplessness of the dependent unemployed, who believe that they can no longer control their environment.

Such a critique of in-kind assistance is consistent with the economic criticism that in-kind provision is inefficient: if individuals were provided with the cash value of the in-kind assistance, they would use it purchase goods or services which they valued more.

In spite of such criticisms, I will argue that in-kind provision is often the appropriate form of redistributive policy. I have argued that the capacity to form and pursue ends is the fundamental goal to be advanced by redistributive policies. The goods/services provided in kind are essential preconditions to the development of this capacity. Therefore, it is essential to the realization of this fundamental capacity that such goods/services are received by aid recipients.

While fully informed, free individuals might allocate their income optimally to maximize their autonomous capabilities, the disadvantaged face a constant stream of short-term needs which may distort their consumption priorities. Thus, the poor may not be well situated to form an undistorted perspective, independent of the priorities forced on them by contingent events, from which to calculate their optimal consumption. Since (i) the provision of in-kind goods/services is of fundamental importance to redistributive policy; and (ii) the disadvantaged may fail to use additional income assistance to secure such goods/services; therefore (iii) it is often appropriate to provide in-kind assistance when the goods/services provided constitute fundamental preconditions to the acquisition of capabilities.

CONCLUSION

In this study, I have disputed the traditional view that Kant's political theory requires a classic liberal theory of the state. Rather, I have argued, Kant's political theory both permits and requires state intervention to assist the disadvantaged.

The most serious difficulty facing a practical analysis of Kant's politics is the content problem: how is it possible to specify the practical implications of pure principles. In the arguments of the *Rechtslehre*, this problem is rearticulated in the context of the relation of natural to positive law. The content problem in politics can, therefore, be expressed by the question: what requirements and constraints do the principles of natural law exert over the principles of positive law?

I argue that Kant's account of political teleology grounds a faculty of political judgment to address the political content problem. Kant argues that reflective judgment provides the condition allowing us to realize in the external world '[t]he effect [at which we are to aim] according to the concept of freedom' (CJ 195–6). Thus, reflective judgment specifies the practical implications of pure principles. Politics constitutes an important dimension in which the practical implications of pure moral principles are to be realized: 'a true system of politics cannot . . . take a single step without first paying tribute to morality' (TPP 125). This 'tribute to morality' requires the realization of an objective end of reason, the 'highest political good' (MJ 355). Reflective (teleological) judgment makes possible a representation of this objective end that is merely implicit in pure principles of morality.

The specification of this objective end both vindicates the possibility of practical political deliberation and makes possible the identification of the requirements of practical reason in the political and legal spheres. It is the role of objective ends in facilitating the specification of the practical implications implicit in pure principles that leads Kant to describe moral philosophy as 'a pure practical teleology'[25] (GTPP 182–3). Objective ends are, in fact, a necessary condition for morality. If all ends were merely 'means to other ends', there could be no action without an end, and thus 'a *categorical imperative* would be impossible'; therefore, without objective ends, 'the doctrine or morals would be destroyed' (DV 385).

---

[25] '[E]ine reine praktische Teleologie' (GTPP 182–3).

The faculty of political (teleological) judgment permits us to specify the substantive implications of the principles of natural law, and thus makes possible a substantive theory of positive legislation. I argue that Kantian political judgment specifies equal access to the opportunity to develop one's capacity for unconditioned purposiveness as a fundamental principle grounding substantive requirements for positive legislation. If equal opportunity to develop 'the capacity to set oneself an end' is a necessary condition of realizing a rightful civil condition, then the state must work posi-tively to ensure that empirical conditions and the distribution of property do not interfere with the realization of such equal opportunity. Such a requirement simply embodies the commitment to respect for humanity as an end which grounds Kant's entire moral and political theory. While I suggest that the principle of equal opportunity to develop the capacity to realize ends may have varying distributive implications in differing substantive areas and contexts, I argue that the principle has two general substantive implications relevant to social policy. First, income support must be provided to ensure at least minimally adequate living conditions. Second, above this threshold, the marginal value of funds assigned to income support declines relative to the marginal value of funds allocated to compensatory interventions.

REFERENCES

ALLISON, H. (1983). *Kant's Transcendental Idealism*. New Haven, Conn.: Yale University Press.

—— (1990). *Kant's Theory of Freedom*. Cambridge: Cambridge University Press.

—— (1993). 'Kant's Doctrine of Obligatory Ends'. *Jahrbuch für Recht und Ethik*, 1: 7–24.

—— (1995). 'The Gulf between Nature and Freedom and Nature's Guarantee of Perpetual Peace'. *Proceedings of the Eighth International Kant Congress*.

ARENDT, H. (1982). *Lectures on Kant's Political Philosophy*. Chicago: University of Chicago Press.

AUNE, B. (1979). *Kant's Theory of Morals*. Princeton: Princeton University Press.

BARNOW, B. (1987). 'The Impact of CETA Programs on Earnings: A Review of the Literature'. *Journal of Human Resources*, 22: 157–93.

BASSI, L., and ASHENFELTER, O. (1986). 'The Effect of Direct Job Training and Training Programs on Low-Skilled Workers', in S. H. Danziger and D. H. Weinberg (eds.), *Fighting Poverty*. Cambridge, Mass.: Harvard University Press, 133–51.

BECK, L. W. (1960). *A Commentary on Kant's 'Critique of Practical Reason'*. Chicago: University of Chicago Press.

BEINER, R. (1983). *Political Judgment*. Chicago: University of Chicago Press.

—— and BOOTH, W. J. (eds.) (1993). *Kant and Political Philosophy: The Contemporary Legacy*. New Haven: Yale University Press.

BEISER, F. C. (1987). *The Fate of Reason: German Philosophy from Kant to Fichte*. Cambridge, Mass.: Harvard University Press.

—— (1992a). *Enlightenment, Revolution, and Romanticism: The Genesis of Modern German Political Thought, 1790–1800*. Cambridge, Mass.: Harvard University Press.

—— (1992b). 'Kant's Intellectual Development: 1746–1781', in P. Guyer (ed.), *The Cambridge Companion to Kant*. Cambridge: Cambridge University Press, 26–61.

BERNSTEIN, E. (1961). *Evolutionary Socialism*, trans. E. C. Harvey. New York: Schocken Books.

BIELEFELDT, H. (1997). 'Autonomy and Republicanism: Immanuel Kant's Philosophy of Freedom'. *Political Theory*, 25/4: 524–58.

BOOTH, W. J. (1986). *Interpreting The World*. Toronto: University of Toronto Press.

BYRD, S. (1993). 'Two Models of Justice'. *Jahrbuch für Recht und Ethik*, 1: 45–68.

—— (1995) 'The State as a "Moral Person"'. *Proceedings of the Eighth International Kant Congress*.

CARNOIS, B. (1987). *The Coherence of Kant's Doctrine of Freedom*, trans. D. Booth. Chicago: University of Chicago Press.

CASSIRER, E. (1981). *Kant's Life and Thought*, trans. J. Haden. New Haven: Yale University Press.

CHAPMAN, B. (1970). *Police State*. London: Macmillan.

COHEN, G. A. (1989). 'On the Currency of Egalitarian Justice'. *Ethics*, 99: 906–44.

—— (1990). 'Equality of What? On Welfare, Goods and Capabilities'. *Recherches économiques de Louvain*, 56: 357–82.

COHEN, H. (1910). *Kants Begrundung der Ethik*. Berlin: Bruno Cassirer.

DORWART, R. A. (1971). *The Prussian Welfare State before 1740*. Cambridge, Mass.: Harvard University Press.

DUSING, K. (1968). *Die Teleologie in Kants Weltbegriff*. Kant Studien Erganzungsheft 96. Bonn: Bouvier Verlag.

—— (1971). 'Das Problem des hochsten Gutes in Kants praktischer Philosophie'. *Kant-Studien*, 63: 5–42.

DWORKIN, R. (1977). *Taking Rights Seriously*. Cambridge, Mass: Harvard University Press.

—— (1981a). 'What is Equality? Part I: Equality of Welfare'. *Philosophy and Public Affairs*, 10/3: 185–246.

—— (1981b). 'What is Equality? Part 2: Equality of Resources'. *Philosophy and Public Affairs*, 10/4: 283–345.

DYSON, K. (1980). *The State Tradition in Western Europe*. Oxford: Oxford University Press.

EISENBERG, P. (1966). 'From the Forbidden to the Supererogatory: The Basic Ethical Categories in Kant's Tugendlehre'. *American Philosophical Quarterly*, 4: 1–15.

ELSTER, J. (1992). *Local Justice: How Institutions Allocate Scarce Goods and Necessary Burdens*. New York: Russell Sage.

ERLEBACHER, A. (1970). 'How Regression Artifacts in Quasi-Experimental Evaluations Can Mistakenly Make Compensatory Education Look Harmful', in J. Hellmuth (ed.), *Disadvantaged Child*. New York: Brunner/Mazel.

FLETCHER, G. (1987). 'Law and Morality: A Kantian Perspective'. *Columbia Law Review*, 87/3: 421–32.

FORSTER, E. (ed.) (1989). *Kant's Transcendental Deductions: The Three*

'*Critiques' and the 'Opus Postumum'*. Stanford, Calif.: Stanford University Press.

FRICKE, C. (1990). 'Explaining the Inexplicable: The Hypothesis of the Faculty of Reflective Judgment in Kant's Third Critique'. *Nous*, 24/1: 45–63.

GALSTON, W. A. (1975). *Kant and the Problem of History*. Chicago: University of Chicago Press.

GIBBONS, S. (1994). *Kant's Theory of the Imagination*. Oxford: Clarendon Press.

GINSBORG, H. (1990). 'Reflective Judgment and Taste'. *Nous*, 24: 63–78.

GOLDMAN, B., FRIEDLANDER, D., and LONG, D. (1986). *California: Final Report on the San Diego Job Search and Work Experience Demonstration*. New York: MDRC.

GOLDMAN, L. (1971). *Immanuel Kant*, trans. Robert Black. London: New Left Books.

GREGOR, M. (1963). *Laws of Freedom*. Oxford: Basil Blackwell.

—— (1988). 'Kant's Theory of Property'. *Review of Metaphysics*, 41: 757–87.

—— (1991). 'Translator's Introduction', in I. Kant, *The Metaphysics of Morals*, trans. Mary Gregor. Cambridge: Cambridge University Press.

—— (1993). 'Kant on Obligation, Rights and Virtue'. *Jarbuch für Recht und Ethik*, 1: 69–102.

—— (1995). 'Natural Right or Natural Law'. *Jarbuch für Recht und Ethik*, 3: 11–35.

GUYER, P. (1979). *Kant and the Claims of Taste*. Cambridge, Mass.: Harvard University Press.

—— (1990). 'Reason and Reflective Judgment: Kant on the Significance of Systematicity'. *Nous*, 24: 17–43.

—— (1991). 'Natural Ends and the End of Nature: Reply to Aquila'. *Southern Journal of Philosophy*, 30 (Suppl.): 157–166.

—— (ed.) (1992). *The Cambridge Companion to Kant*. Cambridge: Cambridge University Press.

—— (1993*b*). 'Thought and Being: Hegel's Critique of Kant's Theoretical Philosophy', in P. Guyer (ed.), *The Cambridge Companion to Hegel*. Cambridge: Cambridge University Press, 171–210.

HAYEK, F. A. (1973). *Law, Legislation and Liberty. i: Rules and Order*. Chicago: University of Chicago Press.

—— (1976). *Law, Legislation and Liberty. ii. The Mirage of Social Justice*. Chicago: University of Chicago Press.

HENRICH, D. (1992). *Aesthetic Judgment and the Moral Image of the World: Studies in Kant*. Stanford, Calif.: Stanford University Press.

HENRICH, D. (1994). *The Unity of Reason*. Cambridge, Mass,: Harvard University Press.

HERMAN, B. (1990). *Morality as Rationality*. New York: Garland.

—— (1993). *The Practice of Moral Judgment*. Cambridge, Mass.: Harvard University Press.

HILL, T. E. (1989). 'Kantian Constructivism in Ethics'. *Ethics*, 99: 752–70.

—— (1991). *Autonomy and Self-Respect*. Cambridge: Cambridge University Press.

—— (1992). *Dignity and Practical Reason in Kant's Moral Theory*. Ithaca, NY: Cornell University Press.

HOFFE, O. (1978). *Ethik und Politik: Grundmodelle und Probleme der praktischen Philosophie*. Frankfurt am Main: Suhrkamp Verlag.

—— (1992). ' "Even a Nation of Devils Needs the State": The Dilemma of Natural Justice', in H. L. Williams (ed.), *Essays on Kant's Political Philosophy*. Chicago: University of Chicago Press, 120–42.

—— (1994). *Immanuel Kant*. Albany, NY: State University of New York Press.

HUMBOLDT, W. von (1969/1852). *The Limits of State Action*, trans. J. W. Burrow. Cambridge: Cambridge University Press.

JUSTI, J. H. G. (1755). *Staatswirthschaft, oder Systematische Abhandlung aller Oekonomischen und Cameral-Wissenschaften*. Leipzig: B. C. Breitkopf.

—— (1756). *Kurzer systematischer Grundriss aller Oeconomischen und Cameralwissensschaften*. Leipzig: Gesam. Pol. u. Finanzschriften.

—— (1759). *Der Grundriss einer Guten Regierung*. Frankfurt and Leipzig.

KERSTING, W. (1984). *Wohlgeordnete Freiheit: Immanuel Kants Rechts- und Staatsphilosophie*. Berlin: Walter de Gruyter.

—— (1992a). 'Kant's Concept of the State', in H. L. Williams (ed.), *Essays on Kant's Political Philosophy*. Chicago: University of Chicago Press, 143–65.

—— (1992b). 'Politics, Freedom, and Order: Kant's Political Philosophy', in P. Guyer (ed.), *The Cambridge Companion to Kant*. Cambridge: Cambridge University Press, 342–66.

KORSGAARD, C. (1985). 'Kant's Formula of Universal Law'. *Pacific Philosophical Quarterly*, 66: 24–47.

—— (1986). 'Kant's Formula of Humanity'. *Kant-Studien*, 77/2: 183–202.

—— (1989). 'Morality as Freedom', in Y. Yovel (ed.), *Kant's Practical Philosophy Reconsidered*. Boston: Kluwer, 23–48.

—— (1990). *The Standpoint of Practical Reason*. New York, NY: Garland.

—— (1992). 'Creating the Kingdom of Ends: Reciprocity and Responsibility in Personal Relations', in J. Tomberlin (ed.), *Philosophical Perspectives 6: Ethics, 1992*. Atascadero, Calif.: Ridgeview.

—— (1996*a*). *Creating the Kingdom of Ends*. Cambridge: Cambridge University Press.

—— (1996*b*). *The Sources of Normativity*. Cambridge: Cambridge University Press.

LONGUENESSE, B. (1995). 'The Transcendental Ideal and the Unity of the Critical System'. *Proceedings of the Eighth International Kant Congress*.

LONGUENESSE, B. (1998). *Kant and the Capacity to Judge: Sensibility and Discursivity in the Transcendental Analytic of The Critique of Pure Reason*. Princeton: Princeton University Press.

MCFARLAND, J. D. (1970). *Kant's Concept of Teleology*. Edinburgh: University of Edinburgh Press.

MAKKREEL, R. A. (1990). *Imagination and Interpretation in Kant*. Chicago: University of Chicago Press.

—— (1991). 'Regulative and Reflective Uses of Purposiveness'. *Southern Journal of Philosophy*, 30 (Supplement): 49–71.

MULHOLLAND, L. (1990). *Kant's System of Rights*. New York: Columbia University Press.

MURPHY, J. G. (1970). *Kant: The Philosophy of Right*. London: Macmillan.

NEIMAN, S. (1994). *The Unity of Reason*. Oxford: Oxford University Press.

—— (1995). 'Understanding the Unconditioned'. *Proceedings of the Eighth International Kant Congress*.

O'NEILL (NELL), O. (1975). *Acting on Principle*. New York: Columbia University Press.

—— (1989). *Constructions of Reason*. Cambridge: Cambridge University Press.

OSSE, M. (1717/1556). *Testament*. Leipzig.

PIPPIN, R. (1982). *Kant's Theory of Form*. New Haven: Yale University Press.

—— (1985). 'On the Moral Foundation of Kant's *Rechtslehre*', in R. Kennington (ed.), *The Philosophy of Immanuel Kant*. Washington, DC: Catholic University Press.

—— (1991). 'Hegel, Ethical Reasons, Kantian Rejoinders' *Philosophical Topics*, 19/2: 99–132.

—— (1995). 'Avoiding German Idealism: Kant and the Reflective Judgment Problem'. *Proceedings of the Eighth International Kant Congress*.

PLUHAR, W. S. (1987), 'Translator's Introduction', in W. S. Pluhar (trans.), *Critique of Judgment*. Indianapolis: Hackett, xxiii–cix.

POGGE, T. (1988). 'Kant's Theory of Justice'. *Kant-Studien* 79: 407–33.

RAWLS, J. (1971). *A Theory of Justice*. Cambridge, Mass.: Harvard University Press.

—— (1980). 'Kantian Constructivism in Moral Theory'. *Journal of Philosophy*, 77: 515–72.

RAWLS, J. (1989). 'Themes in Kant's Moral Philosophy', in E. Forster (ed.), *Kant's Transcendental Deductions: The Three 'Critiques' and the 'Opus Postumum'*. Stanford, Calif.: Stanford University Press, 81–113.

—— (n.d.). 'Lectures on Kant's Moral Philosophy'. Cambridge, Mass.: Unpublished MS.

REATH, A. (1989*a*). 'Hedonism, Heteronomy and Kant's Principle of Happiness'. *Pacific Philosophical Quarterly*, 70: 42–72.

—— (1989*b*). 'Kant's Theory of Moral Sensibility: Respect for Moral Law and the Influence of Inclination'. *Kant–Studien*, 80: 284–302.

RILEY, P. (1983). *Kant's Political Philosophy*. Totowa, NJ: Rowman & Littlefield.

—— (1992). 'Hannah Arendt on Kant, Truth and Politics', in H. L. Williams (ed.), *Essays on Kant's Political Philosophy*. Chicago: University of Chicago Press, 305–23.

ROSEN, A. D. (1993). *Kant's Theory of Justice*. Ithaca, NY: Cornell University Press.

ROSENBLUM, N. (1987). *Another Liberalism*. Cambridge, Mass.: Harvard University Press.

SANDEL, M. (1982). *Liberalism and the Limits of Justice*. Cambridge: Cambridge University Press.

SCHNEEWIND, J. B. (1997). 'Introduction', in P. Health and J. B. Schneewind (eds.), *Lectures on Ethics*. Cambridge: Cambridge University Press, xiii–xxvii.

—— (1998). *The Invention of Autonomy*. Cambridge: Cambridge University Press.

SECKENDORFF, L. (1675). *Teutscher Fürsten Stat*. Frankfurt: T. M. Gotzens.

SEN, A. (1980). 'Equality of What', in S. McMurrin (ed.), *The Tanner Lectures on Human Values*, vol. i. Cambridge: Cambridge University Press, 195–220.

—— (1985). 'Well-being, Agency and Freedom: The Dewey Lectures of 1984'. *Journal of Philosophy*, 82: 169–221.

SHELL, S. (1980). *The Rights of Reason: A Study of Kant's Philosophy and Politics*. Toronto: University of Toronto Press.

SILBER, J. R. (1962). 'The Importance of the Highest Good in Kant's Ethics'. *Ethics*, 73: 179–97.

—— (1959). 'Kant's Conception of the Highest Good as Immanent and Transcendent'. *Philosophical Review*, 68: 469–92.

SMALL, A. (1909). *The Cameralists*. New York: Burt Franklin.

SULLIVAN, R. S. (1989). *Immanuel Kant's Moral Theory*. Cambridge: Cambridge University Press.

TAGGART, R. (1981). *A Fisherman's Guide: An Assessment of Training and Remediation Strategies*. Kalamazoo, Mich.: W. E. Upjohn.

VAN DER LINDEN, H. (1988). *Kantian Ethics and Socialism*. Indianapolis: Hackett.

VAN PARIJS, P. (1991). 'Why Surfers should be Fed: The Liberal Case for an Unconditional Basic Income'. *Philosophy of Public Affairs*, 20: 101–31.

VORLANDER, K. (1902). 'Die neukantische Bewegung im Sozialismus'. *Kant-Studien*, 7: 23–84.

WEINRIB, E. (1987). 'Law as a Kantian Idea of Reason'. *Columbia Law Review*, 87/3: 472–508.

—— (1992). 'Law as Idea of Reason', in H. L. Williams (ed.), *Essays on Kant's Political Philosophy*. Chicago: University of Chicago Press, 15–49.

WILLIAMS, B. (1985). *Ethics and the Limits of Philosophy*. Cambridge, Mass.: Harvard University Press.

WILLIAMS, H. (1983). *Kant's Political Philosophy*. New York: St Martin's Press.

—— (ed.) (1992). *Essays on Kant's Political Philosophy*. Chicago: University of Chicago Press.

WOLFF, R. P. (1973). *The Autonomy of Reason: A Commentary on Kant's Groundwork of the Metaphysics of Morals*. New York: Harper & Rowe.

WOOD, A. W. (1989). 'The Emptiness of the Moral Will'. *Monist*, 73: 454–83.

—— (1970). *Kant's Moral Religion*. Ithaca, NY: Cornell University Press.

YOVEL, Y. (1980). *Kant and the Philosophy of History*. Princeton: Princeton University Press.

ZAMMITO, J. H. (1992). *The Genesis of Kant's Critique of Judgment*. Chicago: University of Chicago Press.

INDEX